Authentic Intelligence in Education

Authentic Intelligence in Education

Reclaiming Real Learning in the Age of AI

Katie Alaniz

BLOOMSBURY ACADEMIC
NEW YORK • LONDON • OXFORD • NEW DELHI • SYDNEY

BLOOMSBURY ACADEMIC
Bloomsbury Publishing Inc, 1359 Broadway, New York, NY 10018, USA
Bloomsbury Publishing Plc, 50 Bedford Square, London, WC1B 3DP, UK
Bloomsbury Publishing Ireland, 29 Earlsfort Terrace, Dublin 2, D02 AY28, Ireland

BLOOMSBURY, BLOOMSBURY ACADEMIC and the Diana logo are trademarks of Bloomsbury Publishing Plc

First published in the United States of America 2026

For legal purposes the Acknowledgments on p. xii constitute an extension of this copyright page.

A catalog record for this book is available from the Library of Congress

ISBN: HB: 978-1-4758-7501-0
PB: 978-1-4758-7502-7
ePDF: 979-8-8818-6815-4
eBook: 978-1-4758-7503-4

Typeset by Integra Software Services Pvt. Ltd.

For product safety related questions contact productsafety@bloomsbury.com.

To find out more about our authors and books visit www.bloomsbury.com and sign up for our newsletters.

This book is dedicated to the glory of God.

Contents

Preface

The guidebook you hold in your hands resulted from numerous personal and professional experiences over the past several decades. I first encountered the impact of authentic learning with digital tools and resources, particularly authentic assessment, while pursuing a Master of Education at Houston Christian University (formerly Houston Baptist University) in Houston, Texas. Dr. Dawn Wilson, the architect behind the university's M.Ed. in Curriculum and Instruction with a Specialization in Instructional Technology program, designed and supervised this transformative experience.

Dr. Wilson's courses inspired students to "begin with the end in mind" (Covey, 1989), facilitating the development of authentic projects through diverse technologies, preparing her students for successful careers in education within the digital age. Throughout the program, students created online portfolios that highlighted their learning accomplishments, along with various other practical applications. At the end of each semester, Dr. Wilson's students regularly shared their pride in their newfound knowledge and skills, eagerly seeking to showcase their learning artifacts. These growth opportunities significantly enhanced students' personal and professional effectiveness, greatly influencing their teaching practices.

Even before attending HCU, during nearly a decade of teaching first and second grade in public and private schools, I noticed heightened student engagement and eagerness to learn when digital tools were meaningfully integrated into lessons. In 2009, aiming to harness the potential of instructional technology more effectively, I enrolled in HCU's M.Ed. in Curriculum and Instruction with a Specialization in Instructional Technology program.

Under Dr. Wilson's guidance, I became aware of the vast range of digital tools and resources that could enhance authentic learning experiences. After each class session, I was eager to implement the new technological skills I learned in my second-grade classroom, and my students always responded enthusiastically.

As one example, my second graders were captivated by a Claymation video I created as an assignment in my graduate program to help them understand cardinal directions in social studies. At the end of the video, they wholeheartedly applauded and asked to watch the video again and again. Experiences like this occurred regularly during my graduate studies, further solidifying my confidence in the effectiveness of strategically and authentically integrating instructional technology. These moments inspired me to continually seek authentic, applicable, innovative ways to incorporate technology into teaching.

After earning my Master of Education and beginning a doctoral program in learning, design, and technology, I became a digital learning specialist at my school while also working part-time as an elementary computer instructor. Inspired by Dr. Wilson's dedication to educational excellence and her investment in students' growth as individuals and professionals, I joined the faculty of HCU's College of Education and Behavioral Sciences shortly after completing my doctorate. This role has provided me with numerous opportunities to implement the authentic learning methods that Dr. Wilson modeled over a decade ago in her M.Ed. program.

Thanks to Dr. Wilson's mentorship, I have seen increased student engagement, motivation, and success through deliberate learning initiatives that connect with real-life situations and link to students' current and future personal and professional aspirations. Inspired by Dr. Wilson's exemplary practices, I feel a responsibility as an educator to ensure my students' time in school is well-spent, especially considering the countless hours they dedicate to furthering their education.

This guidebook is the result of established frameworks for meaningful living and growing (Covey, 1989; Sinek, 2011; Wiggins and McTighe, 2005), integrating essential principles from previous books focusing on the intentional pursuit of impactful authentic learning (Alaniz, 2021; Alaniz, 2024; Alaniz and Cerling, 2023; Alaniz and Wilson, 2015; Wilson, Alaniz, and Sikora, 2016).

Having experienced the transformative impact of authentic learning and meaningful assessments (as well as endured ineffective assessment methods as a student and an educator), I am committed to empowering others to embrace authentic learning practices. As an educator who has taught in various settings, from first grade to graduate courses, I have witnessed the power of authentic learning to heighten student engagement and inspire learners to achieve their fullest potential.

I have found that when my students and I focus less on completing academic "to-dos" and instead reflect more on "why we engage in our work," educational experiences become increasingly fulfilling and joyful. Teaching and learning should be meaningful and exciting. Together with my students, I have discovered that authentic learning is crucial for purpose-driven and joyful teaching; I hope the same holds true for my readers. Authentic learning brings out the best in educators and their students, ultimately infusing genuine excitement into learning experiences.

As the field of education adapts to ongoing societal shifts and technological transformations, one of the most profound changes we now face is the impact and integration of artificial intelligence (AI). My foundation in authentic learning, combined with over a decade of experience in curriculum design and instructional technology, has uniquely prepared me to engage with this next chapter in educational innovation.

In my current role at Houston Christian University, I have had the immense privilege of designing and teaching courses for the Learning, Technology, and Design programs—courses that actively explore how emerging technologies, including AI, can be used to foster purposeful, learner-centered experiences. These opportunities have deepened my understanding of how AI can amplify, not replace, authentic teaching strategies, helping educators personalize instruction, streamline feedback, and create space for more profound human connection in learning environments.

This book is a product of those experiences. It seeks to bridge timeless principles of authentic learning with the transformative potential of AI. Rather than positioning artificial intelligence as a threat to traditional teaching, I offer this resource as a way to thoughtfully embrace AI as a tool—one that, when guided by sound pedagogy and human-centered values, can enhance the depth and relevance of education in remarkable ways.

In Honor of Dr. Wilson …

On September 9, 2019, Dr. Wilson transitioned from this world to her eternal home after courageously battling cancer for five years. Throughout her lifetime and into her final moments, she exemplified extraordinary courage, an unwavering sense of hope, and an unquenchable passion for her calling as an educator. Even in her last days, she skillfully supported her colleagues and guided her students to achieve their goals.

Dr. Wilson's life and legacy inspired the creation of this book. The content within it serves as a tribute to this exceptional educator and remarkable individual. Through the privilege of knowing her, my life and teaching practices have been profoundly enriched.

References

Alaniz, K. (2021). *Collegial Coaching: Mentoring for Knowledge and Skills That Transfer to Real-World Applications*. Bloomsbury.

Alaniz, K. (2024). *A Learning Community Built on Strengths: Inspiring Educators to Positively Impact Student Lives*. Bloomsbury.

Alaniz, K. and D. Wilson (2015). *Naturalizing Digital Immigrants: The Power of Collegial Coaching for Technology Integration*. Bloomsbury.

Alaniz, K. and K. Cerling (2023). *Authentic Assessment in Action: An Everyday Guide for Bringing Learning to Life through Meaningful Assessment*. Bloomsbury.

Covey, S.R. (1989). *The 7 Habits of Highly Effective People: Restoring the Character Ethic*. Free.

Sinek, S. (2011). *Start with Why*. Penguin.

Wiggins, G. and J. McTighe (2005). *Understanding by Design* (2nd ed.). Pearson/Merrill Education/ASCD.

Wilson, D., K. Alaniz, and J. Sikora (2016). *Digital Media in Today's Classrooms: The Potential for Meaningful Teaching, Learning, and Assessment*. Bloomsbury.

Acknowledgments

I offer my deepest gratitude to my incredible husband, Steven,
my everyday hero and greatest cheerleader.
Your unwavering love and enduring support have made all the difference.
To my loving family and cherished friends:
thank you for being a constant source of strength, encouragement, and joy.
Your faithful prayers have carried me through each new venture,
and I am forever grateful for your steadfast support.
I extend special appreciation to the educators who first
lit the spark of my passion for teaching—in
particular, Dr. Dawn K. Wilson—professor, mentor, and dear friend,
whose wisdom and inspiration helped shape many of the ideas in this book.
Lastly, I honor my very first teachers—my brilliant and loving parents.
Your example, guidance, and love laid the foundation for everything I am.

Introduction

The significant expansion of artificial intelligence (AI) has transformed how individuals access, interpret, and generate content, more than at any point in human history. Innovations fueled by AI are reshaping nearly every industry, and education is no exception. Today's students effortlessly tap into vast amounts of information through the devices at their fingertips. While knowledge acquisition still plays a crucial role, students now require support in navigating, filtering, and applying the information they access, particularly in a world where AI can both assist and overwhelm.

The growing presence of AI prompts many crucial questions for educators to consider, including:

- How can educators guide learners in meaningfully utilizing AI for learning and for life without diminishing their content knowledge and creative abilities?
- How can educators leverage AI to facilitate students' transition from consumers of information to creators of new learning experiences?
- How can educators design learning experiences that transfer beyond classroom settings and prepare students for life outside of school, both now and for years to come?

By leveraging authentic learning as a means of "beginning with the end in mind" and designing educational experiences that apply to everyday life, educators empower students to utilize the tools of the age, including AI, to grow and innovate. Even as they devote increasing time and energy to consuming information, many students struggle with deficient digital literacy skills and a lack of awareness of digital safety. Educators today have the opportunity and responsibility to guide learners in using AI as a tool for deeper thinking, not just faster completion.

Authentic Intelligence in Education: Reclaiming Real Learning in the Age of AI is a guidebook designed to inspire educators with practical strategies and innovative ideas for integrating authentic learning with technology, including AI, in classroom settings. His book presents an innovative framework designed to equip educators (and ultimately their students) not only to survive but to undeniably thrive in the age of AI.

Chapter 1 explores how artificial intelligence is revolutionizing the delivery of relevant and meaningful learning experiences. In a world where information is no longer scarce, students face a new set of challenges: discerning credibility, applying knowledge in complex digital contexts, and maintaining originality in an environment where AI can generate ideas instantly. This chapter explores how authentic learning serves as a necessary response to these shifts. Rather than focusing solely on academic performance, students increasingly seek experiences that feel purposeful and connected to their futures. As learners navigate evolving academic and professional landscapes influenced by AI, this chapter encourages educators to design learning opportunities that foster autonomy, inquiry, and long-term engagement.

Chapter 2 examines the evolving role of artificial intelligence in transforming educational environments and informing instructional decision-making. As AI tools become increasingly embedded in both academic and everyday contexts, educators face new questions about how to design meaningful learning experiences that reflect these shifts. This chapter highlights the growing influence of AI on how students interact with content, how teachers design instruction, and how learning is assessed. It provides an overview of emerging trends, historical context, and key considerations that can help educators navigate this changing landscape with clarity and purpose.

Chapter 3 emphasizes the foundational role of course goals, student learning outcomes, and learning objectives in shaping instruction and assessment. In light of AI's expanding presence in education, this chapter provides practical strategies for articulating clear learning targets that remain relevant in a rapidly evolving environment. This chapter explores approaches to designing outcomes that support purposeful integration of AI tools while reinforcing essential skills and knowledge. Attention is also given to helping students understand the value of these objectives and connect them to real-world applications and future professional settings influenced by AI.

Chapter 4 offers practical guidance for selecting and implementing a range of assessment strategies suited to today's dynamic learning environments. It considers both assessments that purposefully integrate artificial intelligence and those that encourage learning without relying on digital tools. Educators will find reflective questions and adaptable ideas to support the development of assessments that are both relevant and responsive to student needs. This chapter emphasizes how authentic learning principles can be applied across assessment types to promote deeper engagement and meaningful demonstration of understanding.

Chapter 5 highlights the lasting impact that well-designed assessment experiences can have on student learning, especially at a time when the availability of AI tools makes it easier for students to disengage from the learning process. When assessments align with students' interests and experiences beyond the classroom, they foster deeper motivation and a stronger commitment to producing original work. This chapter presents a framework for designing such assessments, using the formula introduced in *Collegial Coaching: Mentoring for Knowledge and Skills That Transfer to Real-World Applications* (Alaniz, 2021): authentic issues + authentic audiences + authentic assessment = authentic learning experiences.

Building on this model, the chapter provides strategies for posing relevant, real-world problems, creating opportunities for students to interact with varied audiences, and designing assessments that connect meaningfully with students' lives and goals.

Chapter 6 addresses the essential responsibility educators have when introducing artificial intelligence and other digital tools into learning environments. Before implementation, thoughtful consideration must be given to the ethical, practical, and safety-related repercussions of these technologies. This chapter examines the educator's role in helping students become informed, responsible digital citizens. It also outlines strategies for promoting ethical awareness and fostering safe practices as students engage with AI and other digital resources in both academic and everyday contexts.

Chapter 7 provides a concluding reflection on how educators can shift from simply managing change to actively thriving in the evolving educational landscape shaped by artificial intelligence. As students begin to recognize and develop their creative strengths, they also gain a stronger understanding of how classroom learning connects to the world beyond school. This final chapter features real examples and success stories that illustrate the power of authentic learning in environments where AI is increasingly present. These stories are meant to support and inspire educators as they seek to implement meaningful instructional practices. By embracing authentic learning and adapting to the growing influence of AI, educators can create lasting, positive impacts on student engagement, achievement, and long-term growth.

On the Role of AI in the Writing Process

In keeping with this book's theme of exploring artificial intelligence in education, it is important to note that AI-assisted tools were used in its development. These tools supported brainstorming, organizing ideas, and refining the text, while the author retained full creative control. This use is considered AI-assisted, meaning that AI functioned as a supportive tool, comparable to a grammar checker, search engine, or brainstorming aid, rather than serving as the primary creator of the material.

By contrast, AI-generated work refers to content created primarily by AI systems, where large portions of text, analysis, or narrative are produced automatically with minimal human shaping. That distinction matters in education, as it highlights the difference between using AI to enhance human creativity versus using AI to replace it. While disclosure of AI assistance is not required, it is included here in the spirit of transparency and to model responsible, ethical use of AI in educational contexts.

Reference

Alaniz, K. (2021). *Collegial Coaching: Mentoring for Knowledge and Skills That Transfer to Real-World Applications*. Bloomsbury.

1 Foundations for Relevance

Exploring Authentic Learning in an AI-influenced Educational Landscape

"To be innovative, we can't look to what others have done.
The whole idea of blazing a path is that there was no path there before."
SIMON SINEK

As artificial intelligence (AI) reshapes the world at an unprecedented pace, the call for meaningful, human-centered learning has never been more urgent or promising. AI is transforming what it means to deliver relevant and purpose-filled learning experiences. Information is no longer scarce, and today's students encounter new challenges: identifying credible sources, applying knowledge in increasingly complex digital settings, and maintaining originality in an era where AI can generate content in seconds. These shifts prompt educators to reconsider not only what students should learn but also how they learn and why it matters.

In the current digital landscape, AI-driven technologies influence nearly every sector of society, including education. Many individuals now interact with AI daily, often without conscious awareness. For example, AI powers everyday tools such as facial recognition to unlock smartphones, GPS navigation, predictive text, and spellcheck features (Reeves, 2023). These tools have become so embedded in modern life that their presence may go unnoticed, yet their impact on learning environments continues to grow.

Educators are also navigating a broad spectrum of public reactions to AI, ranging from enthusiasm to skepticism. As noted by Brevetti (2024), much like the early concerns surrounding the use of calculators in math instruction, today's debates about AI reflect deeper questions about the purpose of education and the evolving role of technology. While some fear that AI might limit student thinking, others recognize that it can streamline routine tasks, thereby allowing learners to devote greater attention to complex concepts.

The growing presence of AI prompts many crucial questions for educators to carefully consider, including:

- How can educators guide learners in meaningfully utilizing AI for learning and for life without diminishing their content knowledge and creative abilities?
- How can educators leverage AI to facilitate students' transition from consumers of information to creators of new learning experiences?
- How can educators design learning experiences that transfer beyond classroom settings and prepare students for life outside of school, both now and for years to come?

These questions reflect a broader reality. As students continue to engage with AI in their personal and academic lives, they increasingly seek learning experiences that feel purposeful, applicable, and relevant to their futures. This chapter introduces authentic learning as a necessary and timely response to those expectations. When educators create opportunities that promote autonomy, inquiry, and real-world relevance, students transition from being passive recipients of information to active creators and problem solvers.

At the same time, many students struggle with digital literacy and lack a clear understanding of the responsible use of AI tools. Educators are uniquely positioned to guide learners in developing these skills. Rather than avoiding or restricting AI, teachers can help students leverage it to enhance their creativity, critical thinking, and reasoning. In doing so, they create the conditions for sustained engagement, meaningful motivation, and lasting academic achievement.

Educators who embrace this evolving landscape can meet students where they are and support them in becoming more than merely consumers of AI-enhanced content. They hold the potential to empower students in the quest to become responsible creators and ethical users of the digital tools at their disposal. Doing so requires a shift in perspective, one that views AI not as a threat to authentic learning but as a tool that, when intentionally leveraged, can elevate meaningful engagement and innovation in academic settings.

Learners today are not only seeking practical applications of their academic experiences but also expect educational environments to reflect the complexity and pace of the digital world they inhabit. As AI becomes a common presence in their everyday routines, through tools like adaptive search engines, predictive text, and AI chat assistants, students expect to engage with learning experiences that feel both technologically current and personally meaningful.

While foundational competencies such as creativity, collaboration, and critical thinking remain essential, the rise of AI shifts the context in which these skills must be applied. As Fullan and Scott (2014) emphasize, these skills serve as enduring pillars of deep learning. However, their application now requires students to learn how to collaborate not only with peers but also with machines, to think critically about algorithmic outputs, and to communicate ideas that may have been assisted by AI. Digital and global citizenship also take on expanded meaning as students must make ethical decisions about AI applications and digital authorship. In this new landscape, the role of character includes not just integrity but also a nuanced understanding of how to act responsibly in AI-mediated contexts.

The Irrelevance of "Teaching to the Test"

Despite widespread agreement among educators that "teaching to the test" is not the best approach for engaging students or providing quality education, this practice continues in many educational institutions, from kindergarten through twelfth grade and into higher education. How did we end up in a place where so many districts and education institutions feel that test preparation must take center stage?

At the beginning of the twentieth century, public schools adopted various "innovations" in educational methods that reflected the leading learning theories of that era (National Academies of Sciences, Engineering, and Medicine, 2000). These changes emphasized efficiency, with the primary goals centered on ensuring that a large number of students achieved mastery of the essential skills in reading, writing, and arithmetic. As noted in the book *How People Learn* (2000):

> *In the early 1900s, the challenge of providing mass education was seen by many as analogous to mass production in factories. School administrators were eager to make use of the "scientific" organization of factories to structure efficient classrooms. Children were regarded as raw materials to be efficiently processed by technical workers (the teachers) to reach the end product (Bennett and LeCompte, 1990; Callahan, 1962; Kliebard, 1975). This approach attempted to sort the raw materials (the children) so that they could be treated somewhat as an assembly line. Teachers were viewed as workers whose job was to carry out directives from their superiors—the efficiency experts of schooling (administrators and researchers). (p. 132)*

Furthermore, these frameworks significantly shaped assessment strategies and standards, leading to the emergence of a new era, namely the era of standardized testing.

> *The emulation of factory efficiency fostered the development of standardized tests for measurement of the "product," of clerical work by teachers to keep records of costs and progress (often at the expense of teaching), and of "management" of teaching by central district authorities who had little knowledge of educational practice or philosophy (Callahan, 1962). In short, the factory model affected the design of curriculum, instruction, and assessment in schools. (National Academies of Sciences, Engineering, and Medicine, 2000, p. 132)*

In today's world, the knowledge and skills essential for success in modern workplaces differ significantly from those valued over a century ago (Alaniz, 2021; Alaniz, 2024; Alaniz and Cerling, 2023). With the rapid pace of digital innovation, professional environments are evolving more swiftly than ever before, making the continuous reskilling of employees essential in a dynamic job market. As change becomes the only constant, educators face the daunting challenge of preparing learners for future careers that may not even exist for years to come.

The "Six C's" of Learning in the Age of AI

Although educators cannot possibly foresee the specific careers their students will choose in the future, they can create learning opportunities that help students develop essential skills for success in any profession, even those that have yet to be created. Rather than returning to the traditional, one-size-fits-all learning model of the twentieth century, future-focused learning experiences equip students with the capabilities needed to make a meaningful difference in their lives beyond academics (Alaniz, 2021; Alaniz, 2024; Alaniz and Cerling, 2023).

These skills encompass the "Six C's" of learning in the digital era, as initially described in a white paper by Fullan and Scott (2014):

- *Character: "Qualities of the individual essential for being personally effective in a complex world, including grit, tenacity, perseverance, resilience, reliability, and honesty."*
- *Citizenship: "Thinking like global citizens, considering global issues based on a deep understanding of diverse values with genuine interest in engaging with others to solve complex problems that impact human and environmental sustainability."*
- *Collaboration: "The capacity to work interdependently and synergistically in teams with strong interpersonal and team-related skills, including effective management of team dynamics, making substantive decisions together, and learning from and contributing to the learning of others."*
- *Communication: "Mastery of three fluencies: digital, writing, and speaking tailored for a range of audiences."*
- *Creativity: "Having an 'entrepreneurial eye' for economic and social opportunities, asking the right questions to generate novel ideas, and demonstrating leadership to pursue those ideas into practice."*
- *Critical Thinking: "Critically evaluating information and arguments, seeing patterns and connections, constructing meaningful knowledge and applying it in the real world." (pp. 6–7)*

Learners in the digital age intuitively desire educational experiences that are both applicable and practical. They envision a future professional environment that values transferable skills applicable across diverse academic and career settings. A 2018 study by Dell Technologies and the Institute for the Future (IFTF) projects that 85 percent of the jobs that will exist in 2030 have not yet been invented. In a labor market increasingly shaped by automation and artificial intelligence, students will be expected to work alongside intelligent systems, rather than simply following static procedures.

As AI takes on more technical and repetitive tasks, the value of human contributions will shift toward uniquely human abilities: problem-solving, empathy, ethical decision-making, and adaptability. Educational systems must therefore prioritize learning experiences that nurture these capabilities, preparing students to enter fields that will likely evolve even as they participate in them.

The Importance of Starting with WHY

In his thought-provoking book *Start with Why: How Great Leaders Inspire Everyone to Take Action*, Sinek (2011) emphasizes that while most organizations can effectively express WHAT they do, and many can clearly define HOW they stand out or improve upon competitors, only a select few can essentially convey WHY they exist.

Given the practical mindset of today's students, their desire to learn and grow increases significantly when they understand the purpose behind their learning and growth (Alaniz, 2021; Alaniz, 2024; Alaniz and Cerling, 2023). Whether inside or outside the classroom, relevant and meaningful activities foster enduring growth among today's learners, encouraging even the initially reluctant to step out of their comfort zones. Before embarking on any new path, students see immense benefit in knowing the reason behind their anticipated investment of time and effort. Educators, much like leaders in any organization, sustain long-term success and inspire innovation in their students' learning experiences by focusing on purpose over productivity.

At the beginning of a course or a new lesson, educators enhance student success by clearly defining goals and empowering students to do the same. By starting with the end goal in mind and understanding the purpose behind it, they foster authentic engagement and compelling learning experiences. When teachers articulate a clear vision of student outcomes before initiating new learning endeavors, students are much more inclined to work toward achieving these goals. It is imperative that educators offer their students more than just a list of tasks; they should equip them with an understanding of why each learning opportunity is valuable.

As in any area of life, educational journeys that lack a clear purpose fail to inspire students' intrinsic motivation to persist when challenges and unexpected setbacks arise (Alaniz, 2021; Alaniz, 2024; Alaniz and Cerling,

2023; Wilson, Alaniz, and Sikora, 2016). When educators, and consequently their students, dedicate time to thoughtfully considering a meaningful goal, they dispel the fog and light the way toward a definitive endpoint—a destination that resonates with real-world relevance. With a clear purpose in mind, their intrinsic motivation to persevere fuels their drive to the finish line.

As described by Wilson, Alaniz, and Sikora (2016), this process may be likened to physical journeys in life:

> *Just as travelers embark on journeys with a vision for the final destination as their driving focus, effective educators map curriculum with a clear picture of what students should ultimately know or be able to do at the forefront of their minds. Such teachers design authentic assessment pieces in light of pre-determined standards, thus confirming that these assessments will ultimately gauge the extent to which students have achieved desired learning outcomes. (p. 115)*

Questions such as the following support students in actively articulating and reflecting on the WHY:

- What is the rationale behind our investment of time and energy in this unit of learning?
- What motivates us to passionately engage with and apply this content?
- Beyond the basic answer that "Mastery of this content is essential for achieving an A on the exam or in the course," what significance does this unit or lesson hold?

Starting with WHY remains a critical practice in instructional design. However, in the era of artificial intelligence, this practice gains new urgency. Students now have instant access to information, answers, and even AI-generated responses. This abundance of content heightens the need for learning experiences that clearly communicate their relevance. When educators frame content with a clear sense of purpose, helping students understand not just what to learn but why it matters in a technology-driven world, they equip learners to engage with both curiosity and discernment. Understanding the WHY is no longer a motivational strategy alone; it is essential for navigating a world in which content can be replicated instantly, but meaning cannot.

Beginning with the End in Mind

"Beginning with the end in mind," a principle articulated by Covey (1989), remains a powerful tool in instructional planning. In the context of artificial intelligence, this practice now includes an added layer of intentionality. Educators must consider not only the learning goals but also how students might engage with AI tools to meet those goals. This may include developing outcomes that specify when and how AI tools can be ethically integrated to support the learning process. In this way, beginning with the end in mind becomes not just a matter of defining success, but of preparing students to utilize emerging technologies to achieve that success with integrity and insight.

The upcoming chapters emphasize the importance of beginning with the end in mind and starting with WHY as essential principles in creating meaningful, innovative, and relevant learning experiences.

Leveraging AI to Design Student-Centered Learning Experiences

Educators hold the potential to leverage AI to foster meaningful, memorable, learner-centered approaches, empowering students to start with WHY and begin with the end in mind in their educational pursuits. Students naturally seek to explore a wide array of subjects and discover significance in their learning. They will likely engage with AI in their future careers, and educators hold the potential to more effectively prepare them for the future by equipping them today to make informed decisions and to prepare for success in an AI-driven world (Brevetti, 2024).

In the words of Brevetti,

> *In a not-too-distant past, math teachers complained that calculators would make students worse at basic arithmetic. They projected that students would not be able to make calculations through mental math or even lose the ability to put pen to paper. When I worked as a carhop in high school, we were not allowed to carry calculators, and no one fathomed that one day we would have a calculator right on our cell*

phone in our pocket! So, what really happened? Calculators saved people from mundane calculations which facilitated learners to progress more proficiently to complex math. (para. 4)

Although the rise of artificial intelligence is often linked to the twenty-first century, it emerged in the early 1950s. However, leasing a computer at that time could cost as much as $200,000, since these machines were still sizable and not widely used (Kapur, 2023). As a result, only wealthy universities and tech companies could explore the potential of AI for the future.

In today's educational landscape, both educators and students can readily explore concepts with a variety of learning devices, especially since smartphones now seem like an extension of students' hands (Brevetti, 2024). A crucial question emerges in an increasingly digital world: When is it appropriate to incorporate AI and technology in the classroom while maintaining a balance between human interaction and computational intelligence?

Brevetti (2024) insightfully offers the following answer to this question:

The aspect of the learning process under focus will determine whether we practice computational or human skills. In projects that involve resource gathering, fact-checking, and brainstorming challenging issues, AI can enhance authentic teaching and learning. Experiences that foster group collaboration, hands-on projects, and emotional intelligence development typically require little technological intervention. Our students are intricate individuals with diverse backgrounds and emotions, and AI is incapable of fully understanding these emotions. Furthermore, GIGO is a popular computer term for "Garbage In, Garbage Out" to show that data fed into a system might be incorrect. In this fast-paced world, it's often necessary to help our learners figure out what is accurate and what their purpose is as they find their way. Technology will never replace what a teacher does to inspire and guide students. (paras. 10–11)

Today's learners yearn for educational opportunities that prompt them to reflect on the purpose behind their learning and to envision their goals from the outset. They seek relevant experiences that enable them to apply and enhance their existing knowledge and skills, effectively positioning them to make a meaningful impact in future professional environments, even in uncertain situations. Assessment strategies play a crucial role in equipping students for forward-thinking learning experiences that extend beyond the classroom and into their lives.

Teacher-Created Versus Student-created Learning Strategies

Some educators lean toward a teacher-centric learning environment, assuming their students will learn through similar methods that their teachers used decades ago. When educators anticipate that students will acquire knowledge the same way they did during their own educational experiences, this phenomenon may be described as a "generational gap in teaching" or "teaching informed by personal learning experiences."

In such cases, teachers may inadvertently implement pedagogical strategies that were effective for them as learners, potentially disregarding the diverse needs and learning preferences of today's student population, a population that necessitates more contemporary and flexible approaches.

Student-centered learning proves to be more effective than teacher-centered approaches because it actively involves students in their own learning process (Alaniz, 2021; Alaniz, 2024). By promoting active participation, this approach deepens comprehension and strengthens critical thinking.

In some cases, teachers inadvertently revert to teacher-centered learning strategies when they block the use of digital tools and resources, such as AI, out of fear of losing control of the classroom if students rely too heavily upon such technologies to complete assignments, potentially diminishing learning opportunities while facilitating cheating.

Ultimately, restricting AI due to such fears will not genuinely benefit students in the long term. Learning is enhanced as educators adopt a forward-thinking perspective, ensuring that students utilize technology meaningfully in today's classrooms while preparing for success in higher education and their future professions.

In the words of Roberti (2024),

> *Imagine a future where people don't understand the most potent tool shaping our economy, society, and daily lives. If we don't adequately prepare the next generation, that possibility will quickly become our reality. Artificial intelligence (AI) isn't a distant innovation; it's an integral part of our daily existence. In this new reality, we must ask: Are schools preparing the next generation to understand and responsibly use this transformative technology? In many classrooms, the answer is no. Embedding AI into school curriculums is essential because AI is already embedded in our world, influencing everything from health care and finance to education and entertainment. Without equipping students with AI literacy, we risk leaving them unprepared for the job market and unable to navigate the ethical questions or political issues of AI. (para. 1)*

AI has already had a significant effect on workforce dynamics and this influence is expected to continue increasing in the coming years. The International Monetary Fund reports that artificial intelligence is expected to affect roughly three out of every five positions across the United States and other developed economies (Roberti, 2024), with the percentage of affected jobs across various industries expected to continue rising.

AI-driven automation is currently transforming various sectors, including manufacturing and customer service, where numerous tasks that were historically assigned to individuals are now being executed by automated systems. Without a comprehensive understanding of artificial intelligence, students may encounter difficulties securing employment in an economy that is progressively dependent on this technology (Roberti, 2024).

Future professions will increasingly emphasize the importance of leveraging AI to create rather than merely consume. This involves employing technological innovations not only to access information or content passively, but also to actively generate new ideas, designs, texts, or other creative outputs. Therefore, AI will primarily serve as an instrument that aids in innovative processes, rather than merely as a means of consumption for pre-existing material. When today's educators guide students in harnessing AI to engage in creation rather than solely focusing on consumption, they more effectively prepare them to navigate and excel in the professional landscapes of the future. Such creative endeavors are at the heart of student-centered learning.

The importance of teacher-centered versus student-centered learning becomes especially clear when considering assessment strategies. When educators consider the varying effectiveness of different assessment types, one important factor to reflect on is who designed the assessment. Assessments designed by students can have a significantly different impact than those crafted exclusively by educators.

As described by Alaniz and Cerling (2023),

> *In a teacher-centered assessment model, teachers exclusively identify, create, and evaluate. Other than taking an assessment, students have no involvement in the assessment process, and likely, little involvement in the learning process. In a student-centered assessment model, students create as a means of demonstrating their own learning. In this model, students have greater ownership in their learning and academic progress. When students are active participants in assessment, they are able to self-monitor their own learning and to monitor their learning gaps. (pp. 15–16)*

The subsequent sections of this guidebook highlight the value of authentic, student-centered learning, integrated with digital tools and resources—including AI—to help educators and students forge meaningful connections between educational endeavors and real-world applications beyond the classroom. While more conventional assessment methods, such as multiple-choice quizzes and examinations, limit students' opportunities to cultivate the "Six C's" of learning in the digital era, authentic learning prioritizes the advancement of these skills.

The table below, created by the Center for Innovative Teaching and Learning at Indiana University Bloomington (2022), highlights important distinctions between traditional and authentic learning strategies.

Typical Tests	Authentic Tasks	Indicators of Authenticity
Require correct responses	Require a high-quality product or performance and a justification of the solutions to problems encountered	Correctness is not the only criterion; students must be able to justify their answers.
Must be unknown to the student in advance to be valid	Should be known in advance to students as much as possible	The tasks and standards for judgment should be known or predictable.
Are disconnected from real-world contexts and constraints	Are tied to real-world contexts and constraints; require the student to "do" the subject	The context and constraints of the task are like those encountered by practitioners in the discipline.
Contain items that isolate particular skills or facts	Are integrated challenges in which a range of skills and knowledge must be used in coordination	The task is multifaceted and complex, even if there is a right answer.
Include easily scored items	Involve complex tasks that for which there may be no right answer, and that may not be easily scored	The validity of the assessment is not sacrificed in favor of reliable scoring.
Are "one shot"; students get one chance to show their learning	Are iterative; contain recurring tasks	Students may use particular knowledge or skills in several different ways or contexts.
Provide a score	Provide usable diagnostic information about students' skills and knowledge	The assessment is designed to improve future performance, and students are important "consumers" of such information.

Effective educational opportunities motivate educators and students to explore the reasons behind learning, envision desired outcomes, and connect academic experiences to real-life contexts. This approach embodies authentic learning, fostering engagement and inspiration in learners as they develop the knowledge and skills for future success, preparing to make a positive impact on the world.

And that is what this book is all about: in an AI-driven world where information is abundant but true understanding must be actively built, authentic learning is no longer optional. It is essential. By fostering creativity, relevance, and active participation, educators can move beyond compliance-focused teaching toward inquiry-based, real-world learning that provides students with the skills, mindsets, and ethical grounding to navigate complex issues with confidence and purpose. The chapters that follow will delve deeper into this vision, drawing on current research, insights from leading educational experts, and real-world examples to illustrate how authentic learning can thrive in an AI-enhanced educational landscape.

Essential Ideas to Remember

In a time defined by rapid progress in artificial intelligence, the importance of authentic learning has never been greater. AI has permeated daily life, influencing how individuals access, process, and create information. For educators, this presents both challenges and opportunities. Rather than resisting AI, educators more effectively prepare their students for the future by leveraging AI as a tool to enhance learning experiences, ensuring that students transition from simply consuming information to actively creating knowledge and understanding.

Traditional teaching models, particularly the "teaching to the test" approach, are increasingly irrelevant in preparing students for the modern world. Originating from early twentieth-century ideals of industrial efficiency, standardized testing emphasizes rote memorization rather than critical thinking and problem-solving. However, today's learners require adaptable skills to navigate an increasingly complex and ever-evolving workforce. Studies suggest that the majority of jobs expected in the coming decades have not yet been created, underscoring the necessity for flexible, transferable competencies.

To address this, educators should emphasize the "Six C's" of learning in the digital age: character, citizenship, collaboration, communication, creativity, and critical thinking (Fullan and Scott, 2014). These skills not only prepare students for diverse career paths but also foster innovation and global engagement. Today's learners value education that is both meaningful and applicable to real-world scenarios. They seek experiences that go beyond test scores, focusing on creativity, ethical decision-making, and the ability to adapt to complex challenges.

Key aspects of authentic learning include beginning with the end in mind and starting with WHY, principles that empower students to establish clear goals and understand the purpose behind their learning. When students grasp the relevance of their learning, their motivation and engagement naturally increase, resulting in a deeper understanding and longer-term retention.

While AI can assist in information retrieval, brainstorming, and analysis, human interaction remains irreplaceable for developing emotional intelligence, ethical reasoning, and collaborative problem-solving. The key lies in finding balance—using AI to support learning while maintaining a focus on interpersonal connections and hands-on experiences.

Authentic assessment plays a central role in this new learning paradigm. Moving beyond traditional exams, when assessment shifts from a passive evaluation to an ongoing, reflective process, students develop a deeper commitment to their learning journey. It is important for educators to foster a growth mindset, inspiring students to view learning as a continuous process rather than a collection of isolated activities.

Lastly, embracing student-centered learning over teacher-centered instruction is essential for success in the age of AI. Teachers who rely on outdated methods risk alienating students who thrive in interactive, technology-enhanced environments. Instead, fostering an educational setting that values student input, collaboration, and personalized learning paths will better prepare them for the complexities of the modern workforce.

As the digital landscape continues to advance, education must adapt alongside it. By focusing on purpose-driven learning, educators can inspire students to embrace lifelong learning and innovation in an AI-driven world. This approach empowers educators and, ultimately, their students not merely to survive but to effectively thrive in the age of AI.

References

Alaniz, K. (2021). *Collegial Coaching: Mentoring for Knowledge and Skills That Transfer to Real-World Applications*. Bloomsbury.

Alaniz, K. (2024). *A Learning Community Built on Strengths: Inspiring Educators to Positively Impact Student Lives*. Bloomsbury.

Alaniz, K. and K. Cerling (2023). *Authentic Assessment in Action: An Everyday Guide for Bringing Learning to Life Through Meaningful Assessment*. Bloomsbury.
Bennett, K.P. and M.D. LeCompte (1990). *The Way Schools Work: A Sociological Analysis of Education*. Longman.
Brevetti, M. (2024, March 27). *(Re)Imagining AI for Educators: How to Improve Learner-centered Classrooms with Futuristic Possibilities*. Faculty Focus. https://www.facultyfocus.com/articles/teaching-with-technology-articles/reimagining-ai-for-educators-how-to-improve-learner-centered-classrooms-with-futuristic-possibilities/.
Callahan, R.E. (1962). *Education and the Cult of Efficiency*. University of Chicago Press.
Covey, S.R. (1989). *The 7 Habits of Highly Effective People: Restoring the Character Ethic*. Free.
Dell Technologies (2018). *Realizing 2030: A Divided Vision of the Future*. https://bit.ly/2FvF1yi.
Fullan, M. and G. Scott (2014). *New Pedagogies for Deep Learning Whitepaper: EducationPLUS*. Collaborative Impact SPC.
Indiana University Bloomington (2022). *Authentic Assessment*. Center for Innovative Teaching and Learning. https://citl.indiana.edu/teaching-resources/assessing-student-learning/authentic-assessment/index.html.
Kapur, R. (2023). *AI Made Simple: A Beginner's Guide to Generative Intelligence*. Rinity Media.
Kliebard, H.M. (1975). "Metaphorical Roots of Curriculum Design." In W. Pinar (ed.), *Curriculum Theorizing: The Reconceptualists* (pp. 84–5). McCutchan.
National Academies of Sciences, Engineering, and Medicine (2000). *How People Learn: Brain, Mind, Experience, and School: Expanded Edition*. National Academies Press. https://doi.org/10.17226/9853.
Reeves, S. (2023). *8 Helpful Examples of Artificial Intelligence*. https://www.iotforall.com/8-helpful-everyday-examples-of-artificial-intelligence.
Roberti, J. (2024, December 3). *Students Must Be Prepared for an AI-dominated Future*. Baltimore Sun. https://www.baltimoresun.com/2024/12/03/students-must-be-prepared-for-an-ai-dominated-future-guest-commentary/.
Sinek, S. (2011). *Start with Why*. Penguin.
Wilson, D., K. Alaniz, and J. Sikora (2016). *Digital Media in Today's Classrooms: The Potential for Meaningful Teaching, Learning, and Assessment*. Bloomsbury.

2 Shifting Ground

Charting AI-driven Changes in Authentic Pedagogy

"We cannot always build a future for our youth, but we can build our youth for the future."
FRANKLIN D. ROOSEVELT

In a world that is increasingly dependent on digital tools and resources for survival and success in various aspects of life, today's educators are acutely aware of the effects of technological innovation, both positive and negative. Now, more than ever, educators face unprecedented opportunities and challenges that their predecessors did not anticipate.

As described in the book *Collegial Coaching: Mentoring for Knowledge and Skills That Transfer to Real-world Applications* (Alaniz, 2021),

> *The lives of today's learners include an abundance of technological tools and resources, providing them unprecedented access to information on any imaginable subject. Consistent digital connectedness allows them to create and instantaneously distribute multimedia content to individuals across the globe. Online social networking opportunities enable learners of the present age to interact with others from various parts of the world, providing them an increasingly broader audience for conveying ideas, collaborating, and learning alongside. Beyond the borders of their school contexts, students enjoy virtually boundless autonomy to follow their passions. For countless learners of today, technical innovations represent immense, instant opportunities. (p. 14)*

The Promises and Pitfalls of Digital Innovation

In an era of digital dependence, innovative educators and educational leaders worldwide are exploring new ways to harness technological advancements to create engaging, relevant, and enduring learning experiences—experiences that extend beyond the classroom and last over time. These opportunities foster knowledge and skills that resonate with learners' daily lives while equipping them for future academic, professional, and personal pursuits.

Instead of designing educational experiences through traditional instructional strategies, a complete transformation of the pedagogical paradigm is necessary. Those who facilitate learning must transition from teacher-centered practices to approaches that actively position students as the drivers of their own learning. When thoughtfully integrated into educational contexts, digital tools and resources can empower learners, enabling them to take charge of their own learning experiences while enhancing flexibility and providing a greater scope for growth and creativity.

As noted by Alaniz (2021),

> *Faced with heightened directives for accountability, many of today's teachers grapple with allocating time in their increasingly packed schedules to research the latest technological innovations, let alone incorporate digital tools and resources within the curriculum. At most, some educators simply integrate technology as a means of checking this "to do" off the list, rather than strategically, intentionally implementing digital tools and resources to modify or redefine learning experiences for students. Encouragement and support in doing so are essential, more so now than ever before in the history of education. (p. 17)*

Artificial intelligence (AI) has become one of the most influential digital innovations today, affecting many fields, including education. More than just a tool for automating routine tasks, AI is increasingly a strategic resource that helps humanity solve complex problems and achieve goals that once seemed impossible. In academic settings, many educators see AI as a powerful way to improve learning, streamline workflows, and embrace the idea of "working smarter, not harder."

The transformative impact of AI, however, goes far beyond classrooms, fostering advances in business, healthcare, science, and many other sectors. For over a decade, AI has led technological progress, boosting efficiency, innovation, and tangible results across various industries. However, these opportunities come with challenges, as the same technologies that enhance productivity and open new possibilities can also introduce ethical dilemmas, reinforce biases, threaten data privacy, and pose risks of overreliance on automated systems. Therefore, understanding AI requires both recognizing its different forms and critically examining its potential drawbacks. One of the most prominent examples of widespread AI use is generative AI (GenAI). This rapidly developing form of machine learning is reshaping many aspects of society (Marr, 2023).

Traditional AI, commonly referred to as "narrow or weak AI," focuses on executing a specific task intelligently. As described by Marr (2023),

> *It refers to systems designed to respond to a particular set of inputs. These systems have the capability to learn from data and make decisions or predictions based on that data. Imagine you're playing computer chess. The computer knows all the rules; it can predict your moves and make its own based on a pre-defined strategy. It's not inventing new ways to play chess but selecting from strategies it was programmed with. That's traditional AI—it's like a master strategist who can make smart decisions within a specific set of rules. Other examples of traditional AIs are voice assistants like Siri or Alexa, recommendation engines on Netflix or Amazon, or Google's search algorithm. These AIs have been trained to follow specific rules, do a particular job, and do it well, but they don't create anything new. (para. 2)*

Alternatively, GenAI can be viewed as the next stage in the progression of AI.

> *It's a form of AI that can create something new. Suppose you have a friend who loves telling stories. But instead of a human friend, you have an AI. You give this AI a starting line, say, "Once upon a time, in a galaxy far away..." The AI takes that line and generates a whole space adventure story, complete with characters, plot twists, and a thrilling conclusion. The AI creates something new from the piece of information you gave it. This is a basic example of generative AI. It's like an imaginative friend who can come up with original, creative content. What's more, today's generative AI can not only create text outputs, but also images, music, and even computer code. Generative AI models are trained on a set of data and learn the underlying patterns to generate new data that mirrors the training set. (Marr, 2023, para. 3)*

The key distinction between traditional AI and GenAI lies in their functions and applications (Marr, 2023). Traditional AI is largely designed to analyze data and make forecasts, while generative AI can generate original outputs that reflect the data on which it was trained. Essentially, traditional AI is skilled at recognizing patterns, while GenAI specializes in creating new patterns. Traditional AI can interpret data and identify what it shows, but GenAI can leverage that data to generate entirely novel outputs (Marr, 2023).

The scope of GenAI is broad, facilitating new opportunities for creativity and innovation (Marr, 2023). In design, it rapidly produces multiple prototypes, making the ideation process more efficient. In entertainment, it helps generate new music, write scripts, and create deepfakes—digitally altered media that convincingly replace one person's likeness with another. In journalism, it can produce articles and reports. GenAI holds the potential to redefine sectors driven by creative and innovative processes. At the same time, traditional AI plays a vital role in specialized applications such as chatbots, recommendation systems, and predictive analytics, forming the backbone of many existing tools that enhance efficiency across diverse sectors (Marr, 2023).

The rapid rise of AI in education introduces both promises and pitfalls. Much like any technological advancement, innovations associated with AI evoke excitement among some individuals while sparking fears in others. As described by Jorgenson (2024),

> *As educators look for ways to leverage AI responsibly, the trend raises a slew of questions, including: Is AI perpetuating bias due to the bias of the developers who build the technology? Does it save educators or students time, and can it help with learning loss suffered from the pandemic? AI is embedded in day-to-day life and evolving incredibly fast. Just as ChatGPT emerged just over a year ago, AI will continue to evolve. Despite the challenges, AI has the potential to not just make menial tasks easier and faster but to provide more targeted learning experiences for students. (para. 4)*

As with many technological advancements throughout history, today's educators approach the integration of AI in education with both caution and anticipation. While concerns persist about potential student misuse, ethical implications, and the risk of job displacement as reliance on AI grows, these apprehensions are often weighed against the technology's capacity to deliver more personalized learning, foster deeper engagement, and prepare students to apply AI responsibly and effectively in their future professional contexts.

Such mixed reactions align with humankind's responses to many technological innovations of the past. Although the word "technology" is commonly associated with digital tools and resources, technology is more broadly defined as the application of knowledge to accomplish everyday goals, particularly in an explicit and reproducible way (Skolnikoff, 1993). By this definition, useful tools that support humankind in achieving practical purposes—including the printing press, the pencil, and the telephone—may reasonably be described as "technological innovations."

Throughout history, humans have exhibited reluctance to adopt new technologies. For instance, the printing press, which revolutionized the global sharing of information, faced a mixed response upon its introduction by Johannes Gutenberg in the fifteenth century. Before the arrival of the printing press, the process of creating books involved painstakingly handwritten copies, which were both expensive and time-consuming. With the advent of the printing press, book publication expanded significantly, enabling many more individuals to access previously unavailable texts.

Despite the significant benefits of the printing press, many strongly resisted this "cutting-edge" invention. In 1492, German abbot Johannes Trithemius wrote the following in a treatise entitled *Praise of Scribes*:

> *Brothers, nobody should say or think, "What is the sense of bothering with copying by hand when the art of printing has brought to light so many important books; a huge library can be acquired inexpensively."... All of you know the difference between a manuscript and a printed book. The word written on parchment will last a thousand years. The printed word is on paper. How long will it last? The most you can expect of a book of paper to survive is two hundred years. Yet there are many who think they can entrust their works to paper. (Knieriem, 1993: 39)*

Throughout history, similar uneasy reactions have emerged regarding various technological innovations, including now-essential inventions like electricity, telephones, and personal computers. As with any emerging technology, AI holds significant potential for positive applications that can greatly benefit society. Nevertheless, it also carries risks such as errors, limited understanding of proper context, and potential bias in its outputs.

It is helpful to remember that technology is neither inherently good nor bad and does not possess a clear understanding or appreciation of the world.

It cannot function like a human due to its inability to comprehend nuances, experience emotions, or handle intricate moral situations. Unlike humans, AI lacks a soul; it is devoid of reasoning and cannot create subjective experiences.

As with other technological advances, the impacts of AI, including its benefits and its challenges, ultimately hinge on the decisions and values of those who shape and govern its use. The upcoming chapters will delve into these benefits and challenges in detail, ultimately providing practical strategies and innovative ideas for utilizing authentic learning methods to enhance technology integration, including AI, in educational settings. The present chapter encourages readers to adopt a goal-oriented mindset by concentrating on essential standards and skills that learners need to effectively navigate and even excel as scholars and future professionals in the age of AI.

Strategic Skills for Learners in the Digital Age

As described by the International Society for Technology in Education, or ISTE (2024), "Today's students must be prepared to thrive in an evolving technological landscape. The student section of the ISTE Standards is designed to empower student voice and ensure that learning is a student-driven process."

Empowered learner. Not surprisingly, learner empowerment sits at the top of ISTE's list of standards for students. More precisely, students of the digital age should "leverage technology to take an active role in choosing, achieving, and demonstrating competency in their learning goals, informed by the learning sciences" (ISTE, 2024).

The importance of cultivating student-centered learning opportunities is unquestionable, and digital innovations provide an endless variety of ways to accomplish this purpose. According to the ISTE (2024), today's students should be exposed to educational experiences that encourage them to "set learning goals, develop strategies leveraging technology to achieve them, and reflect on the learning process to improve learning outcomes."

Additionally, learners should engage in scholarly experiences that empower them to "build networks and customize their learning environments in ways that support the learning process" (ISTE, 2024). Such network-building opportunities may involve collaborations with fellow learners and/or experts in relevant fields, such as through social media, virtual meetings, and similar platforms. They should capitalize on the potential of feedback to improve their practice as learners, using digital tools and resources "to seek feedback that informs and improves their practice and to demonstrate their learning in a variety of ways" (ISTE, 2024).

Furthermore, students should "understand fundamental concepts of how technology works, demonstrate the ability to choose and use current technologies effectively, and [be] adept at thoughtfully exploring emerging technologies" (ISTE, 2024).

Digital citizen. According to ISTE (2024), the second essential set of skills for fostering learning opportunities in today's educational settings involves digital citizenship. Students should "recognize the responsibilities and opportunities for contributing to their digital communities" (ISTE, 2024). More specifically, digital citizenship requires students to "manage their digital identity and understand the lasting impact of their online behaviors on themselves and others and make safe, legal, and ethical decisions in the digital world" (ISTE, 2024).

Furthermore, learners in the digital age should "demonstrate empathetic, inclusive interactions online and use technology to responsibly contribute to their communities," and this includes safeguarding "their well-being by being intentional about what they do online and how much time they spend online" (ISTE, 2024). Learners should also develop the ability to appropriately maintain their digital privacy by taking steps to "protect their digital privacy on devices and manage their personal data and security while online" (ISTE, 2024).

In the words of Alaniz (2021), "Those responsible for guiding younger generations—including today's educators—hold the potential to help build outstanding digital citizens of future years" (p. 20). However, "unless teachers are armed with the knowledge and real-world experience with displaying effective digital citizenship in their personal and professional lives, how will they be able to convey these skills to others?" (Alaniz, 2021, p. 20).

Knowledge constructor. The third set of ISTE (2024) standards encompasses learners' abilities to "critically curate a variety of resources using digital tools to construct knowledge, produce creative artifacts, and make meaningful learning experiences for themselves and others." Along these lines, students should utilize "effective research strategies to find resources that support their learning needs, personal interests, and creative pursuits" (ISTE, 2024).

Students should be able to assess the validity and reliability of the data, media, and resources they encounter in their pursuit of acquiring new knowledge. Moreover, they should learn to curate collections of valid, reliable research and artifacts by employing a variety of strategies. Additionally, rather than simply accumulating more information, they should be empowered to create new learning experiences through purposefully investigating real-life problems, cultivating hypotheses, and pursuing applicable solutions.

As described by Alaniz (2021), in today's world in which "information sources—whether reliable and beneficial or misleading and insufficient—may be easily located through the click of a mouse or the tap of a screen, the importance of acquiring research and information fluency cannot be overstated" (p. 20). Furthermore, "Today's learners are regularly inundated with too much instead of too little information. Therefore, the greatest task comes in interpreting how to utilize the information at hand most effectively, as well as in determining which data to reject" (Alaniz, 2021, p. 20).

Unless educators and other trusted mentors provide learners with direction on obtaining these vital skills, students may encounter significant difficulty in leveraging valid, reliable resources and utilizing information in helpful and meaningful ways. However, educators seeking to equip students with these competencies must themselves be adept at locating, organizing, and evaluating the wealth of information available online. With the advancement of AI, these proficiencies have never been more crucial for teachers and their students.

Innovative designer. The fourth ISTE standard emphasizes the importance of engaging in creative design processes, which is one of the most essential skills for students to develop today, as it is one of the most in-demand skills for future professionals. As described by ISTE (2024), students should be able to apply a "variety of technologies within a design process to identify and solve problems by creating new, useful, or imaginative solutions."

They should be able to employ design processes intentionally as a means of formulating ideas, testing hypotheses, and constructing innovative learning artifacts. Furthermore, they should "develop, test and refine prototypes as part of a cyclical design process" (ISTE, 2024). Finally, learners should display a tolerance of uncertainty, determination, and a willingness to grapple with issues without readily available solutions.

To foster student growth as innovative designers, educators must also develop these skills in their own lives. However, many educators struggle with busy schedules and increasingly scripted curricula, which often leave little room for professional innovation. With growing pressure to "teach to the test," there are sometimes limited opportunities or support for educators to create new strategies or tools to address challenges in their teaching practices.

As explained by Alaniz (2021),

> *Many teachers find themselves filling each day with addressing the required curriculum and instructing students in preparation for standardized assessments; sometimes, limited time remains for truly imaginative, inventive pursuits. In such cases, it is especially challenging to visualize how educators might employ digital tools in classroom contexts to ignite students' imaginations and innovative capabilities. (p. 21)*

Computational thinker. The next skill set, as underscored by ISTE (2024), involves computational thinking. More specifically, students should "develop and employ strategies for understanding and solving problems in ways that leverage the power of technological methods to develop and test solutions" (ISTE, 2024). For example, they should "formulate problem definitions suited for technology-assisted methods such as data analysis, abstract models, and algorithmic thinking in exploring and finding solutions" (ISTE, 2024). Additionally, learners should be skilled at collecting relevant data, utilizing digital tools and resources to evaluate the validity and reliability of the data, and representing key findings to engage in effective problem-solving.

Furthermore, students should develop the ability to deconstruct problems, isolate key components, and create descriptive models to better understand complex systems. Finally, learners should develop an understanding of automation processes, utilizing relevant algorithms to design progressive steps that lead to solutions to problems. Facilitating learning experiences that promote critical thinking skills is crucial. When digital tools and resources are used effectively and purposefully, they significantly aid students in developing their computational thinking skills. In the future, more employers will expect potential hires to utilize these skills through innovative technologies.

Learners eagerly anticipate opportunities to leverage digital tools and resources as they aim to address problems and demonstrate a variety of skills in everyday life. Beyond the time spent in the classroom, many students dedicate a significant portion of their day to playing digital games and interacting with programs designed to challenge their minds and develop computational skills. Naturally, when such opportunities are absent in classroom settings, learners struggle to engage in educational experiences that seem irrelevant to their everyday realities.

> *There sometimes appears to be a gulf between how learners are expected to participate at school, how they challenge their minds outside of the school day, and what they might be required to do upon entering professional contexts. What could happen if increasing numbers of teachers were more comfortable with effectively implementing engaging, interactive digital tools and resources within their lessons? How might this serve to generate innovative connections between classroom experiences, the activities and passions students engage in on their own, and the knowledge and skills they will need to function effectively in the future? (Alaniz, 2021, p. 22)*

Creative communicator. Creative communication exemplifies another vital ISTE (2024) standard for today's learners. Students in today's world should "communicate clearly and express themselves creatively for a variety of purposes using the platforms, tools, styles, formats, and digital media appropriate to their goals" (ISTE, 2024). For example, learners should select suitable digital tools and resources to achieve their goals. Additionally, they should "create original works or responsibly repurpose or remix digital resources into new creations" (ISTE, 2024). They should also communicate complex ideas both clearly and effectively. Finally, they should design and present content that "customizes the message and medium for their intended audiences" (ISTE, 2024).

Innovative digital tools and resources continue to expand individuals' ability to communicate, whether with a colleague in the next room or a collaborator on the other side of the world. "Whereas collaboration was once restricted to the times and locations in which participants could be present physically, people can now collaborate at all hours of each day and from any location, irrespective of geographic locales and time zones" (Alaniz, 2021, p. 23).

As observed by Webster-Smith, Albritton, and Kohler-Evans (2012), "People in organizations unknowingly cry out for meaningful conversations that are positive, fruitful, and constructive. The significance of meaningful conversations is especially critical in schools where administrators and teachers are either working in isolation or at cross-purposes" (p. xii). Just as educators "cry out" for chances to communicate meaningful ideas and to work collaboratively with fellow educators, today's students desire connectedness with one another; opportunities to work collaboratively benefit learners in countless ways.

In an increasingly fast-paced society, many individuals unconsciously follow "paths of least resistance," driven by the need to accomplish as much as possible in a short time. This way of living can lead to a sense of disconnection from others and potentially result in feelings of loneliness. While the reliance on digital tools and resources is often seen as a factor contributing to increased isolation, these technological advancements can also enhance communication and collaboration between educators and their students. Digital resources empower scholars and professionals to collaborate creatively with experts from diverse fields, both within educational environments and beyond (Alaniz, 2021).

Global collaborator. ISTE's (2024) seventh and final standard affirms that learners should "use digital tools to broaden their perspectives and enrich their learning by collaborating with others and working effectively in teams locally and globally." Students should take advantage of digital tools "to connect with peers from a variety of backgrounds, recognizing diverse viewpoints and broadening mutual understanding" (ISTE, 2024). Additionally, today's learners should leverage collaborative technologies to connect with others as they investigate issues from various viewpoints. They should also contribute to collaborative endeavors in meaningful ways, taking responsibility for achieving shared goals.

Throughout the global COVID-19 pandemic, educational institutions worldwide struggled with a sudden shift to remote learning. The abrupt move from face-to-face classes to virtual formats, with little time for preparation, placed immense pressure on educators to teach effectively in these new and unfamiliar environments. The pandemic highlighted the need for educators to be ready to utilize available technologies in innovative and sometimes surprising ways to facilitate meaningful learning opportunities.

Today's educators must possess the ability to transition effortlessly between various instructional delivery methods. The subsequent sections of this book will examine multiple ways in which digital tools and resources, including AI, can be effectively employed within both in-person and virtual learning environments to prepare students for navigating the continually evolving academic and professional landscapes.

As educators design learning experiences that empower students to develop the skills mentioned earlier, they equip learners to excel in evolving academic and professional environments. Future-oriented learning opportunities extend beyond the classroom, encouraging students to utilize digital tools and resources effectively as problem solvers and agents of change, currently and into the future.

Although these standards provide a strong framework, actual implementation often proves more complicated. Although AI holds the capacity to improve teaching practices and personalize learning experiences, applying it in real-world settings presents significant challenges for educators. Teachers frequently face limited time, insufficient planning resources, and unclear district policies, which hinder the effective integration of new tools. Additionally, professional development on AI is inconsistent, leaving many educators feeling unready to make informed instructional decisions.

Access disparities also threaten to hinder widespread adoption, with variations in device availability, internet quality, and software access. Additionally, some teachers worry about being displaced or devalued by automation, especially in environments that emphasize efficiency over pedagogy. Addressing these concerns transparently and proactively is essential to ensure that AI integration supports, rather than diminishes, teacher agency and instructional quality.

Practical AI Integration: Supporting ISTE Standards Through Real-world Learning

While the theoretical benefits of AI are substantial, its true power is evident in its practical applications. The classroom examples below demonstrate how AI tools can support genuine, student-centered learning while aligning with the ISTE Standards for Students (2024).

Writing Revision and Feedback

- *ISTE Standards: Empowered Learner, Knowledge Constructor, Creative Communicator*
- Students utilize AI writing assistants, such as Grammarly or ChatGPT, to generate preliminary feedback on early drafts. Instead of simply accepting the AI's suggestions, students are guided by educators to analyze feedback, reflect on choices, and revise with intention. This process fosters metacognition, reinforces ownership of learning, and enables students to demonstrate writing competency through thoughtful revision.

Historical Roleplay with AI

- *ISTE Standards: Knowledge Constructor, Creative Communicator, Global Collaborator*
- In a high school social studies course, students prompt an AI chatbot to simulate dialogues between historical figures. This creative exercise requires students to evaluate primary sources critically, reflect on their context and ideology, and engage in historical empathy. Students then present or debate interpretations, customizing the format to suit their audience while deepening their conceptual understanding.

Math Tutoring with AI Chatbots

- *ISTE Standards: Computational Thinker, Empowered Learner*
- Using AI-based tutors, students receive scaffolded help in solving math problems. Rather than giving direct answers, these tools guide students through logical reasoning, prompting them to break down problems, explore alternative approaches, and reflect on their strategies. Students track progress, set goals, and iterate, ultimately building both math fluency and independent learning habits.

STEM Prototyping in Maker Labs

- *ISTE Standards: Innovative Designer, Computational Thinker*
- In project-based learning environments, students utilize AI-powered design platforms to rapidly prototype and test solutions to real-world

problems. AI tools generate multiple iterations of student ideas, allowing learners to refine designs through experimentation. As part of the design cycle, students develop resilience, engage in authentic problem-solving, and practice critical analysis of their work.

These examples illustrate how AI can support the ISTE vision of students as self-directed, creative, and critically engaged learners. When thoughtfully integrated, AI tools enhance, not replace, core instructional goals by supporting reflection, personalization, collaboration, and higher-order thinking. More importantly, these applications allow students to transition from consumers of content to creators of knowledge, well-equipped for the demands of a digital world.

From Learning About Technology to Transforming Learning Through Technology

For more than two decades, the ISTE Standards, developed through both research and practitioner insight, have served as a framework for effectively applying technology to support learning across the globe. Since their initial release, the standards have undergone significant evolution, shifting in focus from learning about technology to transforming learning through technology (Sykora, 2024).

As explained by Sykora (2024),

> *The ISTE Standards do not define tech skills. Rather, they are a framework designed to empower lifelong learning by building educator and student agency. They don't focus on digital tools—they are intentionally tool-agnostic—but are instead anchored by instructional strategies and learning design. They are not meant to be siloed in a computer class but to be used across disciplines. The ISTE Standards catalyze authentic, hands-on and applied learning so students can thrive and become problem solvers, communicators, computational thinkers and global citizens in the 21st century. Recent research relying on evidence from peer-reviewed studies shows that use of the ISTE Educator Standards positively affects student learning. (paras. 7–8)*

In a similar vein, this guidebook was intentionally created without solely focusing on the use of any specific AI tool or set of tools. Most likely, within weeks of the book's publication, novel AI tools will have emerged, and the tools considered "cutting-edge" prior to the book's publication will seem comparatively passé. Instead, the chapters within this book provide a framework for facilitating authentic learning experiences that endure over time.

Such learning endeavors reflect tried and true principles of instructional design, such as starting with WHY, beginning with the end in mind, empowering students to transition from consumers of information to creators of new learning experiences, and intentionally preparing today's students for tomorrow's professional landscapes by focusing upon knowledge and skills needed for success, both now and into the future.

Responsible adoption necessitates more than technical comprehension; it also involves ethical awareness, transparency concerning the use of these tools, and the procurement of proper consent. Educational institutions should develop policies that safeguard students' well-being and preserve essential human connections within the learning environment. As educators examine the opportunities and challenges presented by AI, the objective extends beyond merely integrating innovative tools; it encompasses cultivating discerning and empowered learners capable of adapting, creating, and leading. By anchoring the use of technology in ethical principles and genuine inquiry, students will be better equipped for the future and prepared for success in the world that awaits.

Essential Ideas to Remember

In today's digital age, educators face both unprecedented opportunities and challenges due to technological advancements. The wide range of digital tools in educational settings gives learners immediate access to vast information, allowing them to create and share multimedia content, collaborate worldwide, and pursue their passions beyond traditional classrooms. However, integrating technology into learning requires shifting from teacher-centered approaches to student-driven experiences that promote engagement, creativity, and adaptability. Careful implementation of digital resources allows students to assume increased responsibility for their learning while giving educators flexible and innovative teaching methods.

Among the most transformative advancements in recent years is artificial intelligence, particularly GenAI. Although AI offers powerful possibilities to enrich learning, enhance efficiency, and personalize educational experiences, it also introduces challenges related to information accuracy, ethics, and the shifting roles of humans in education. Just as past technological innovations, such as the printing press, faced resistance before becoming acceptable—and even essential—to society at large, AI's integration into education elicits mixed reactions. It is essential to acknowledge that technology, in itself, is neither good nor bad; its influence depends on how it is applied Educators must strive to guide students in using AI responsibly and effectively, enhancing learning rather than replacing critical thinking and creativity.

To prepare students for success in the future, the International Society for Technology in Education (ISTE) has outlined key competencies that learners should possess. Student empowerment is central to these standards, emphasizing the need for learners to set goals, leverage technology strategically, and reflect on their progress. Digital citizenship is another critical component, requiring students to manage their online identities, engage in responsible digital behavior, and balance their technology use to protect their well-being. These skills equip learners to navigate digital environments safely and responsibly.

Furthermore, students must critically evaluate information, build knowledge, and curate trustworthy resources. In a time of information overload, distinguishing between credible sources and misleading content is a vital skill. Learners should be encouraged to move beyond passive information intake by engaging in meaningful research, problem-solving, and creative projects. Educators play an essential role in demonstrating these skills, helping students effectively assess, interpret, and apply knowledge.

Creativity and innovation are also fundamental in today's educational landscape. Students should be given opportunities to design, test, and improve ideas using various technological tools. Solving problems through computational thinking, data analysis, and algorithmic reasoning further prepares students with strategies to address complex challenges. Building these skills will be vital for future careers as digital environments continue to influence professional expectations.

Communication and collaboration remain essential in fostering meaningful connections among students and educators. Digital tools enable learners to articulate their ideas clearly, create original content, and tailor their messages to diverse audiences. Moreover, global collaboration broadens perspectives, enabling students to engage with other learners from a variety of backgrounds and walks of life. Educators can foster these collaborative experiences by guiding students to engage responsibly with digital content and to contribute thoughtfully to discussions and projects within a global context.

References

Alaniz, K. (2021). *Collegial Coaching: Mentoring for Knowledge and Skills that Transfer to Real-World Applications*. Bloomsbury.

International Society for Technology in Education (2024). *Standards•S*. https://www.iste.org/standards/for-students.

Jorgenson, J. (2024, January 23). "How AI and Data Will Change Education in 2024." *Forbes*. https://www.forbes.com/councils/forbescommunicationscouncil/2024/01/23/how-ai-and-data-will-change-education-in-2024/.

Knieriem, K. L. (1993). "Book-Fools of the Renaissance." Occasional papers, University of Illinois at Urbana-Champaign. Graduate School of Library and Information Science, 195 (June).

Marr, B. (2023, July 24). "The Difference Between Generative AI and Traditional AI: An Easy Explanation for Anyone." *Forbes*. https://www.forbes.com/sites/bernardmarr/2023/07/24/the-difference-between-generative-ai-and-traditional-ai-an-easy-explanation-for-anyone/.

Skolnikoff, E.B. (1993). *The Elusive Transformation: Science, Technology, and the Evolution of International Politics*. Princeton University Press. http://www.jstor.org/stable/j.ctt7rpm1.

Sykora, C. (2024, August 2). *A New Approach to Updating the ISTE Standards*. International Society for Technology Integration. https://iste.org/blog/a-new-approach-to-updating-the-iste-standards.

Webster-Smith, A., S. Albritton, and P. Kohler-Evans (2012). *Meaningful Conversations: The Way to Comprehensive and Transformative School Improvement*. Rowman & Littlefield.

3 Purposeful Design
Crafting Learning Goals, Outcomes, and Objectives in AI-enriched Contexts

"It is incredibly easy to work harder and harder at climbing the ladder of success only to realize that it's leaning against the wrong wall."
STEVEN R. COVEY

In an ever-changing instructional landscape, meaningful learning outcomes are crafted by visionary educators who dare to think beyond the present and seek to shape the future. As AI transforms how students engage with information, educators must ensure that curriculum design and assessment methods enable learners to transfer knowledge, think creatively, and reflect critically. Students benefit greatly when educators develop purposeful, measurable learning outcomes that match emerging realities, especially in classrooms influenced by generative AI, digital fluency, and new assessment standards.

Curriculum design begins with purpose. When educators develop a clear vision for where students should arrive before commencing new learning journeys, the likelihood of student engagement and achievement increases significantly. Yet, in many educational contexts, the demands of daily logistics and assessment cycles overshadow the foundational WHY behind student learning endeavors.

In the aforementioned classic, *The 7 Habits of Highly Effective People: Restoring the Character Ethic*, Covey (1989) provides a framework of key principles that effectively apply to countless endeavors in life. Among the most notable of these is Habit 2, which addresses the significance of beginning with the end in mind. This habit seems practical and possibly even obvious; however, many individuals naturally lean toward a short-sighted approach to tackling their to-do lists. Instead of focusing on a vision for the future and goals that are significant to that vision, most people concentrate on one step at a time. Nevertheless, short-sightedness's most considerable drawbacks are a lack of clarity and the inability to ensure that actions lead to desired outcomes.

Individuals who achieve remarkable success often start with the end in mind as they strive to realize their dreams and accomplish their life's work. For instance, Warren Buffett, a prominent business leader and billionaire philanthropist, is recognized for adopting the approach of beginning with the end in mind while leading Berkshire Hathaway. By maintaining a clear vision for the company's future, Buffett effectively guided others in working toward that vision through strategic decision-making.

For example, he was known for implementing long-term investment strategies, which allowed him to concentrate more effectively on the company's enduring success rather than prioritizing short-term gains. Furthermore, Buffett became well-known for deliberately cultivating a strong, positive corporate culture, encouraging those within his company to commit to responsible, ethical practices over the years.

Another prominent example of a leader who achieved success by prioritizing the practice of beginning with the end in mind is Sam Walton, the founder of Walmart. From the company's modest beginnings, Walton remained committed to pursuing his vision for what it should ultimately become. By emphasizing customer satisfaction, focusing on the ability to offer essential and desirable goods at low prices, and fostering an "open door" culture where leadership actively listened to the concerns and ideas of associates, Walton realized his dreams for the company, leading its growth from humble origins to impressive retail achievements.

Framing Learning with Purpose

In the book *Collegial Coaching: Mentoring for Knowledge and Skills That Transfer to Real-World Applications* (Alaniz, 2021), the connection between beginning with the end in mind and Sinek's (2011) now-renowned tenet "start with WHY" is examined from the viewpoint of enhancing professional development practices, particularly for educational professionals. The intersection of these principles also relates to curriculum development and instructional design.

Perceptive and visionary individuals plan for new adventures and future steps in life with their ultimate goal in mind. Just as packing for a trip without thinking about the end destination is unwise, starting a lesson or unit without clear desired outcomes is equally imprudent (Alaniz, 2021).

In his inspiring book *Start with Why: How Great Leaders Inspire Everyone to Take Action*, Sinek (2011) explains,

> *Knowing your WHY is not the only way to be successful, but it is the only way to maintain a lasting success and have a greater blend of innovation and flexibility. When a WHY goes fuzzy, it becomes much more difficult to maintain the growth, loyalty, and inspiration that helped drive the original success. By difficult, I mean that manipulation rather than inspiration fast becomes the strategy of choice to motivate behavior. This is effective in the short term but comes at a high cost in the long term. (p. 50)*

Expanding on this principle within educational contexts, Alaniz (2021) emphasizes that

> *when educators develop a clear vision for where students should arrive prior to commencing new learning journeys, the likelihood that students will take action to reach this destination increases significantly ... Unfortunately, far too many educational systems, and the teachers within them, pack each day with busywork that fails to bring students closer to the overarching goals and corresponding objectives. Many educators unknowingly become so caught up in daily to-do lists that they have little time left to think about the purpose behind their work or the tasks at which their students are laboring away each day. In cases such as this, teachers and their students might begin to feel as though they are traveling down a path without purpose; journeys without the WHY eventually begin to seem murky and arduous. (p. 72)*

Clarifying Learning Goals, Outcomes, and Objectives

Even in the age of AI, educators should never feel pressured to cram digital tools and resources into a lesson or unit simply for the sake of using technology. Rather, key curricular goals, outcomes, and objectives should guide all aspects of every learning experience, including the integration of digital tools and resources. Ultimately, the most effective, meaningful, and memorable educational journeys involve an investment of time, effort, and energy from educators in answering questions such as:

- *Why are you teaching this unit?*
- *Why are you passionate about this content?*
- *Beyond answers such as "This content is mandated by the state or district," why is this unit or lesson important for students to learn?*
- *Why should students care about learning this content? (Alaniz, 2021, pp. 72–3)*

After careful reflection on WHY-centric questions like those above, additional questions to ponder as educators begin with the end in mind include:

- *What overarching goals should students obtain through this unit?*
- *What corresponding objectives should students grasp through this unit?*
- *What artifacts of learning might students create to demonstrate that they have mastered the knowledge and skills addressed within these goals and objectives? (Alaniz, 2021, p. 73)*

Incorporating the principles of beginning with the end in mind and starting with WHY takes on renewed significance in an era shaped by artificial intelligence. As digital tools and innovations emerge at a rapid pace, educators must anchor their work in purpose-driven planning, ensuring that technology is used to support learning rather than dictate it. While AI may shift how content is delivered or assessed, what students need to learn remains paramount. Designing impactful, future-ready instruction begins with selecting a curriculum model that supports both human insight and AI-enhanced strategies. The frameworks introduced in the following sections provide practical, evidence-based guidance for educators navigating this evolving landscape.

Integrating the Understanding by Design Framework

Created by Jay McTighe and Grant Wiggins (2011), the Understanding by Design (UbD) framework provides a research-driven, effective approach to planning meaningful and relevant teaching and learning experiences. It is built on several core principles, including:

1. *Learning endeavors are enhanced when educators purposefully contemplate curricular planning.*
2. *In curriculum design and teaching, the focus should be placed on the elevation and extension of student understanding, as well as their ability to transfer learning to future pursuits (for example, the ability to meaningfully employ content knowledge and corresponding skills).*
3. *Understanding is revealed when students receive opportunities to autonomously make sense of new learning, eventually demonstrating acquired knowledge and skills through real-world applications.*
4. *Effective curriculum planning incorporates a framework known as "backward design."*
    - **a** *First, educators should identify desired results for their students. Through the process, the following preliminary questions should be contemplated: Ultimately, what should learners know and be able to do? Along these same lines, which overarching standards must be addressed?*
    - **b** *Teachers should also establish a set of learning goals to work toward. This includes pinpointing key enduring understandings that will remain with students long after the lesson or unit has concluded.*
    - **c** *Educators must also consider what evidence of learning students will be required to demonstrate. The identified evidence of learning should entail specific strategies for evaluating the extent to which students have acquired the necessary knowledge and skills.*
    - **d** *Finally, a plan for learning must be developed. This plan should encourage teachers and their students to begin with the end in mind; this road map will serve as a guide toward achieving the ultimate destination, or the goals established from the outset. (Alaniz, 2021, pp. 73–4)*

The UbD framework, when thoughtfully implemented, equips educators to navigate the complexities of AI-integrated classrooms by maintaining a clear focus on learning outcomes. In a landscape where digital tools, including AI, can easily divert instruction off course, UbD reinforces the idea that technology should serve the curriculum, not become its own curriculum.

This approach encourages educators to treat AI, like textbooks, as a resource rather than the foundation of instruction. It also helps prevent the rise of activity-driven or AI-generated tasks that lack meaningful alignment with learning goals.

UbD calls educators to prioritize what matters most: authentic, transferable learning grounded in real-world relevance. In AI-rich environments, this model becomes even more critical, ensuring that human-centered instruction remains at the core. When implemented with fidelity, UbD supports both teachers and students in creating purpose-driven, engaging, and ethically grounded learning experiences that effectively utilize emerging technologies.

Reimagining Bloom's Taxonomy for AI-Enhanced Learning

Curriculum development in the age of AI must go beyond static standards and embrace dynamic, skill-based learning that prepares students for real-world challenges. One powerful tool to guide this shift is Bloom's Taxonomy, which helps educators structure learning experiences that move from foundational recall to high-level creation and evaluation.

In AI-integrated classrooms, Bloom's framework becomes especially valuable in distinguishing between tasks best handled by machines, such as information retrieval or summarization, and those that demand human judgment, creativity, and critical thinking. Effective instructional design utilizes Bloom's levels to scaffold student progress toward complex learning outcomes, while also incorporating opportunities for learners to collaborate with AI tools to deepen their understanding, personalize learning pathways, and produce innovative work.

By aligning AI use with the cognitive complexity of Bloom's levels, educators ensure that students are not only consuming information but also actively applying, analyzing, and creating in ways that reflect meaningful, future-ready learning. Established by Dr. Benjamin Bloom in 1956, Bloom's Taxonomy provides a clear and concise classification strategy for learning objectives that teachers can establish for their students.

In the words of Alaniz (2021),

Preferably, this classification method should be incorporated throughout instructional and learning cycles as students acquire the content in increasingly complex ways. Distinguishing key, diverse learning goals or objectives aligns with the process of identifying desired results in the Understanding by Design framework. At this point, teachers decide what students should eventually know and be able to do. Learning at higher levels of the taxonomy is dependent on having attained prerequisite knowledge and skills at lower levels. A goal of effective instruction involves moving students from the lower levels of the taxonomy to the higher levels in order to encompass true content area learning.

The levels are as follows:

- *Remembering: recalling basic facts, concepts, and answers*
- *Understanding: comparing, interpreting, or providing descriptions and key ideas*
- *Applying: solving problems in new situations by using acquired facts, techniques, and rules pertaining to the content at hand*
- *Analyzing: formulating inferences and generalizations about the topic while relating it to previously learned content*
- *Evaluating: validating ideas, making judgments, and defending perspectives based on criteria and evidence pertaining to content*
- *Creating: restructuring content into a novel pattern or framework. (pp. 76–7)*

In contemporary educational environments, numerous digital tools and resources are available to support educators and students in their learning pursuits. The ever-growing variety of technological tools designed to enhance learning can feel overwhelming, and identifying the most effective ways to use them to engage tech-savvy learners presents unique challenges (Alaniz, 2021). "Not every lesson must include digital tools and resources. In fact, selecting technological tools and trying to make them fit within a unit or lesson is a prime example of placing the cart before the horse, as the saying goes" (Alaniz, 2021, p. 77).

Curricular design frameworks, focused clearly on acquiring essential content knowledge and skills, should be a top priority before integrating digital tools and resources into units and lessons as appropriate. This sequence significantly simplifies instructional technology integration, allowing educators to utilize digital innovations as a means of learning rather than as the primary driver of new learning experiences (Alaniz, 2021).

The Importance of Meaningful Learning Outcomes in an AI-Driven Era

The intentional design of student learning outcomes remains a cornerstone of effective curriculum development, particularly in classrooms that are increasingly influenced by artificial intelligence. Grounded in the principles of beginning with the end in mind and starting with WHY, clear and measurable outcomes ensure that technology enhances rather than distracts from the core purpose of learning. Frameworks like Understanding by Design and Bloom's Taxonomy continue to offer powerful guidance for educators seeking to balance technological innovation with purposeful instruction.

While learning goals provide a broad vision of the desired impact within a course or program, student learning outcomes define the specific knowledge and skills students should acquire by the conclusion of a lesson, unit, or module. In AI-integrated environments, these outcomes serve as essential guideposts for ensuring that the use of digital tools supports rather than replaces deep cognitive engagement.

As part of UbD, McTighe and Wiggins (2011) offer a process for identifying priorities within a curriculum. This begins with educators reflecting on three core questions—questions that remain deeply relevant even as AI reshapes how content is accessed and applied:

- **What should participants hear, read, view, explore, or otherwise encounter?**

  This question helps educators identify content knowledge worth introducing, including multimedia and AI-generated resources. However, in the hierarchy of content priorities, this level represents surface learning, or information that supports a more profound understanding but is not the goal in itself.

- **What knowledge and skills should participants master?**

  This category encompasses competencies that are essential for student success, including research methods, analytical processes, and domain-specific skills. In AI-enhanced settings, mastery might include the ethical use of AI tools, prompt engineering, or evaluating AI-generated content for accuracy.

- **What are the big ideas and essential understandings that participants should retain?**

  These enduring understandings reflect what students should carry forward beyond the course—concepts that transfer across disciplines and contexts. In a world of instant answers and algorithm-driven personalization, these understandings help students interpret, evaluate, and apply knowledge meaningfully, regardless of the tools available.

This process aligns with Stage 1: Desired Results of the UbD model, a critical step before considering assessment (Stage 2) or learning activities (Stage 3). In classrooms influenced by AI, maintaining this clarity is essential to prevent a shift toward technology-led instruction and to ensure that learning continues to guide how technology is used.

By engaging deeply with these questions, educators can identify the core content and skills that matter most and translate them into high-impact student learning outcomes. These outcomes provide a clear framework for curriculum alignment, instructional planning, and formative assessment, all while enabling flexibility in how students demonstrate mastery, including with the help of AI tools.

Effective learning outcomes clearly define measurable expectations for what students should understand and be able to achieve by the end of a course or program. They prevent the drift toward "checking boxes" and instead foster intentionality, focus, and data-informed instructional decisions. In AI-rich environments, these outcomes also provide a basis for determining when, how, and why AI tools should be used to support, rather than substitute for, student thinking.

Paired with Bloom's Taxonomy, educators can use action verbs aligned to different cognitive levels (remembering, understanding, applying, analyzing, evaluating, creating) to write outcomes that reflect varying depths of learning. For example, students might analyze AI-generated content for accuracy or create original arguments supported by AI-assisted research tools. Including observable behaviors and clear assessment criteria ensures both human and AI-supported learning is measurable, meaningful, and transferable.

Stanny (2016) provides a master list of action verbs for crafting learning outcomes using Bloom's Taxonomy; this list includes the following action verbs associated with each level of the taxonomy:

- *Remember: Cite, define, describe, identify, label, list, locate, match, memorize, name, outline, recall, recite, recognize, record, relate, repeat, reproduce, select, state*
- *Understand: Classify, compare, convert, defend, describe, discuss, distinguish, estimate, explain, express, extend, generalize, identify, infer, interpret, locate, paraphrase, predict, recognize, report, restate, review, rewrite, summarize, translate*
- *Apply: calculate, choose, compute, construct, demonstrate, dramatize, employ, illustrate, interpret, manipulate, modify, operate, practice, prepare, produce, relate, schedule, show, sketch, solve, use*
- *Analyze: Appraise, categorize, classify, compare, contrast, criticize, diagram, differentiate, discriminate, distinguish, divide, examine, infer, outline, point out, question, relate, select, separate, subdivide, test*
- *Evaluate: Appraise, argue, assess, choose, compare, conclude, criticize, critique, defend, estimate, evaluate, judge, manage, prepare, rearrange, reconcile, set up, synthesize*
- *Create: Arrange, assemble, combine, compose, construct, create, design, develop, devise, formulate, generate, invent, modify, organize, plan, prepare, produce, rate, revise, write*

Verbs such as these provide a jumping-off point through which to develop student learning outcomes that correspond with each of the levels of Bloom's Taxonomy. Shabbir (n.d.) offers numerous examples of student learning outcomes aligned with each level of the taxonomy, including the following:

Examples of Bloom's Taxonomy Learning Objectives: **Remember**

- *By the end of this lesson, students will be able to **define** acceleration.*
- *By the end of this lesson, students will be able to **outline** various stages of design thinking.*
- *By the end of this lesson, students will be able to **label** different parts of the human brain.*
- *By the end of this lesson, students will be able to **list** various kinds of loops in JavaScript.*
- *By the end of this lesson, students will be able to **name** different parts of the nervous system. (para. 10)*

Examples of Bloom's Taxonomy Learning Objectives: **Understand**

- *By the end of this lesson, students will be able to **explain** how sensory receptors in our brain detect stimuli.*

- *By the end of this lesson, students will be able to* ***recognize*** *different types of number sequences.*
- *By the end of this lesson, students will be able to* ***explain*** *how the heart pumps blood throughout our body.*
- *By the end of this lesson, students will be able to* ***distinguish*** *between mass and weight.*
- *By the end of this lesson, students will be able to* ***discuss*** *the factors that affect the solubility of a liquid. (para. 12)*

Examples of Bloom's Taxonomy Learning Objectives: **Apply**

- *By the end of this lesson, students will be able to* ***compute*** *their annual pocket money using this mathematical formula.*
- *By the end of this lesson, students will be able to* ***use*** *this accounting software for their annual family budget.*
- *By the end of this lesson, students will be able to* ***forecast*** *the annual revenue of any company using its past data.*
- *By the end of this lesson, students will be able to* ***show*** *how to demonstrate emotional intelligence during an interview. (para. 14)*

Examples of Bloom's Taxonomy Learning Objectives: **Analyze**

- *By the end of this lesson, students will be able to* ***differentiate*** *between differential and inferential statistics.*
- *By the end of this lesson, students will be able to* ***compare and contrast*** *prokaryotic and eukaryotic cells.*
- *By the end of this lesson, students will be able to* ***illustrate*** *how DNA code translates into RNA code.*
- *By the end of this lesson, students will be able to* ***analyze*** *information in the marketing research.*
- *By the end of this lesson, students will be able to* ***analyze*** *how leaves change colors during the fall season. (para. 16)*

Examples of Bloom's Taxonomy Learning Objectives: **Evaluate**

- *By the end of this lesson, students will be able to* ***explain*** *which kind of medicine is better for leukemia and why.*
- *By the end of this lesson, students will be able to* ***defend*** *their proposed hypotheses.*
- *By the end of this lesson, students will be able to* ***assess*** *the environmental impact of coal mining.*

- *By the end of this lesson, students will be able to* ***measure*** *the effectiveness of project-based learning.*
- *By the end of this lesson, students will be able to* ***appraise*** *the practice of social media advertising in business. (para. 18)*

Examples of Bloom's Taxonomy Learning Objectives: **Create**

- *By the end of this lesson, students will be able to* ***develop*** *an application for the Google Play Store.*
- *By the end of this lesson, students will be able to* ***create*** *financial statements in MS Excel.*
- *By the end of this lesson, students will be able to* ***compose*** *the scientific name of an organism.*
- *By the end of this lesson, students will be able to* ***make*** *their own battery charger. (para. 20)*

Ultimately, student learning outcomes should focus on developing complex skills and knowledge. By incorporating Stage 1 of the Understanding by Design framework and Bloom's Taxonomy into the development of learning outcomes, educators can support learners in more fully grasping what they need to accomplish to meet the desired results.

Applying the ABCD Method

The University of California Merced (UC Merced) Teaching Commons (2024) offers a practical procedure for developing attainable, specific, and measurable student learning outcomes utilizing the ABCD structure. As previously noted, while a goal represents a broader vision regarding the overall impact upon students that an educator desires to achieve through a course or program, student learning outcomes (and even more specific lesson objectives) denote more precise, concrete ways to attain those goals.

When considering and articulating lesson objectives attached to students' learning outcomes, the ABCD structure [Audience, Behavior, Conditions, Degree (of Performance)] provides a clear roadmap (UC Merced, 2024).

- *Audience: The student is the audience (The student will (TSW) . . .)*
- *Behavior: The action the student will take to demonstrate understanding/ mastery (e.g., create, analyze)*

- *Condition: Note any special conditions of the performance (e.g., given a set of data; using Python)*
- *Degree: Any specific level of performance desired (e.g., a minimum of three examples)*

The following is a sample goal, outcome, and objective statement provided by UC Merced (2024):

- *Course Goal: To develop as a scholar in the discipline.*
- *Student Learning Outcome: Develop a research paper, including a complete literature review, and write in the style of the discipline.*
- *Student Learning Objective: Given a selected research topic, TSW present findings and cite at least twelve research sources according to the guidelines in Chicago Style Manual, 11th edition or later.*
    - *Audience: TSW . . .*
    - *Behavior: Present findings and cite research sources . . .*
    - *Conditions: Given a selected research topic . . .*
    - *Degree: At least twelve . . . using Chicago Style Manual . . .*

While the UbD framework, Bloom's Taxonomy, and the ABCD method provide effective strategies for mapping course goals, student learning outcomes, and lesson objectives, even the most skillfully written goals, outcomes, and objectives lack impact for learners unless accompanied by the WHY.

Students often struggle to remain motivated in their learning when they cannot understand the importance of their time and effort. However, when educators clearly communicate goals, outcomes, and objectives alongside relevant discussions about their real-life applications, students naturally become more motivated to engage and stick with even the most challenging learning experiences.

Progressing with a Clear Purpose

When students feel uncertain about why they are expected to engage with a unit or lesson, what will be required of them throughout the learning experience, or how they will be evaluated, educational endeavors seem more like arduous obstacle courses than exciting adventures. Engagement, motivation, and success increase when students clearly grasp and articulate these key learning components from the outset.

Stoeckle (n.d.) provides the following guide for helping students engage in vital, proactive reflection before starting a unit or lesson, including the following questions, considerations, and table:

1 ***Purpose***—*Why is my instructor giving me this assignment? How will completing this assignment benefit my learning?*

- ***Skills***: *What skills will I practice?*

  Tip: Consider skills that are both essential to your success in this course and beyond this course [in school/in this field/in professional life/ . . .].

- ***Knowledge***: *What is the content knowledge I will gain by completing this assignment?*

2 ***Tasks***—*What do I need to do and how should I do it?*

- *Is there a logical or required sequence of steps?*
- *Are there common mistakes to avoid?*

3 ***Criteria for Success***—*How do I know I did everything my instructor asked me to do before I turn in my work?*

- *How will I be evaluated?*
- *Is there a checklist or a rubric?*
- *Are there certain format requirements?*

Decipher what is expected of you:

Assignment:
Due Dates:

Purpose
Why do I have to do this assignment? (How does it relate to this class, to my future career?)

Skills Practiced	*Knowledge Gained*
Tasks *What do I need to do? How will I do it?*	
Criteria for Success *How will I be evaluated?*	

Reconsidering Bloom's Taxonomy in the Age of AI

Building on Bloom's Taxonomy, Oregon State University (2024) developed "Bloom's Taxonomy Revisited" as a modern tool for assessing and redesigning course outcomes and student learning, especially in an age influenced by AI. It offers faculty and instructional designers a practical resource to reflect on activities, assessments, and learning outcomes, focusing on the changing interplay between human cognitive skills and AI.

By aligning each level of Bloom's Taxonomy (Remember, Understand, Apply, Analyze, Evaluate, and Create) with corresponding ways AI can support learning, this resource helps educators determine which tasks and skills should be uniquely human and where AI tools can enhance or scaffold the learning process.

The table below (Oregon State University, 2024) encourages thoughtful integration of AI into the curriculum by highlighting:

- How AI can support learners across each cognitive domain by generating examples, providing alternatives, and suggesting improvements

- Which human skills continue to be vital and cannot be replaced, such as ethical judgment, reflection, and social-emotional insight

The framework highlights that, although AI is a valuable addition, it should not substitute the nuanced, creative, and ethical skills that characterize human learning. This view encourages a balanced and deliberate approach to curriculum development, ensuring the distinct value of human cognition is maintained and enhanced. As AI tools continue to develop, regular evaluation of course activities and assessments will be essential to ensure that education remains both meaningful and relevant.

Level	Distinctive Human Skills	How AI Can Supplement Learning
CREATE	Engage in both creative and cognitive processes that leverage human lived experiences, social-emotional interactions, intuition, reflection, and judgment to formulate original solutions	Support brainstorming processes; suggest a range of alternatives; enumerate potential drawbacks and advantages; describe successful real-world cases; create a tangible deliverable based on human inputs
EVALUATE	Engage in metacognitive reflection; holistically appraise ethical consequences of other courses of action; identify significance or situate within a full historical or disciplinary context	Identify pros and cons of various courses of action; develop and check against evaluation rubrics
ANALYZE	Critically think and reason within the cognitive and affective domains; justify analysis in depth and with clarity	Compare and contrast data, infer trends and themes in a narrowly defined context; compute; predict; interpret and relate to real-world problems, decisions, and choices
APPLY	Operate, implement, conduct, execute, experiment, and test in the real world; apply human creativity and imagination to idea and solution development	Make use of a process, model, or method to solve a quantitative or qualitative inquiry; assist students in determining where they went wrong while solving a problem

Level	Distinctive Human Skills	How AI Can Supplement Learning
UNDERSTAND	Contextualize answers within emotional, moral, or ethical considerations; select relevant information; explain significance	Accurately describe a concept in different words; recognize a related example; translate into another language
REMEMBER	Recall information in situations where technology is not readily accessible	Retrieve factual information; list possible answers; define a term; construct a basic chronology or timeline

Leveraging AI to Craft Student Learning Outcomes

AI can support educators' productivity in many areas, including the design of purposeful course goals, student learning outcomes, and objectives that guide learners toward meaningful progress. When provided with appropriate context, AI can generate effective, specific, and measurable targets that align with the desired results of upcoming learning experiences. Educators can then refine these suggestions, adjusting scope and rigor to ensure they are relevant and attainable.

AI tools support instructional design by automating routine tasks, offering personalized feedback, and creating content tailored to student needs. When used effectively, these tools boost efficiency, allowing educators to devote more time to student engagement, formative assessment, and relationship-building (Pappas, 2024). By leveraging AI in the creation of clear, relevant learning goals, outcomes, and objectives, educators can focus more on the human side of teaching, actively engaging with learners and fostering deeper connections.

In crafting effective AI prompts, educators should aim to include specific details about the course, the students in the course, and the course's purpose. This will assist AI in generating goals, outcomes, and objectives that align with the educators' intentions for both the course and the students.

The National Louis University (2024) offers several sample prompts that include very specific information regarding course purposes and the students within the course:

> *Sample Prompt 1 – Course Learning Outcomes: "Help me to write course outcomes for my undergraduate course on healthcare ethics. This will be a 6-week course designed to introduce healthcare students to ethical issues, frameworks, and decision-making processes. Specific topics that we will cover in the course include Patient Rights and Confidentiality, End-of-Life Decision Making, Resource Allocation, Medical Research Ethics, Public Health Ethics, Genetics and Reproductive Ethics, Organ Donation Ethics, and Healthcare Policy. Write a maximum of five course outcomes that encompass these topics. Format my course outcomes as a numbered list. Each outcome should be one sentence. Begin each outcome by using a strong and measurable verb. Use only one verb per objective. Make each outcome student-centered. Avoid using jargon if possible. Don't use the words understand, understanding, demonstrate." (paras. 4–5)*
>
> *Sample Prompt 2 – Module Learning Outcomes: "Help me to write module outcomes for my undergraduate course on healthcare ethics. Here's a list of course outcomes:*
>
> **1** *Evaluate the ethical dimensions of patient rights and confidentiality in healthcare settings.*
> **2** *Justify ethical decisions in end-of-life care, integrating cultural, religious, and legal considerations.*
> **3** *Assess resource allocation in healthcare, focusing on equity and justice in various settings.*
> **4** *Critique ethical challenges in medical research, public health, genetics, and reproductive ethics.*
> **5** *Develop informed positions on organ donation and healthcare policy ethics through research and analysis.*
>
> *I'll be writing module two now. In this module, I want to teach my students about informed consent, access to medical records, disclosure of medical errors, HIPAA compliance and regulations, and patient advocacy and support. Write one module outcome for each of these topics. Format my course outcomes as a numbered list. Begin each outcome by using a strong and measurable verb. Use only one verb per objective. Make each outcome student-centered. Avoid using jargon if possible. Don't use the words understand, understanding, demonstrate. Also, align each of the module outcomes with at least one*

of my course outcomes by including aligned course outcome numbers in parentheses at the end of the module learning outcome." (paras. 7–9)

In addition to the above sample prompts, the following tips and best practices also provide guidance for utilizing AI to craft goals, outcomes, and objectives:

1 ***Review AI Work:*** *As always, it is important for you as the course designer to review and assess learning outcomes generated by AI. Don't just assume that they are correct and that they make sense. Make sure that the objective is suitable for your course, topics, and students.*
2 ***Choose Verbs:*** *While the formatting of learning objectives can change, as a rule of thumb, it's good practice to begin your learning objectives with a strong and measurable action verb. AIs tend to try and use the words "understand" or "demonstrate understanding." However, these are not measurable verbs. It can be helpful to remind the AI not to use these words.*
3 ***Provide Context:*** *In general, the more information that you can provide to your AI, the more likely it is to develop learning outcomes that you can use for your course. Provide as much information as you can upfront about your purpose, learners, topics, course format, and other relevant information. And remember, you can always provide this information later in the conversation and ask the AI to revise the outcomes that it has generated.*
4 ***Use One Verb Per Outcome:*** *AIs tend to be unnecessarily verbose. Consider asking the AI to use only one verb per outcome. This can make outcomes easier to read, understand, and measure. (National Louis University, 2024, para. 11)*

Ultimately, when educators plan with the end goal in mind and lead purposefully, they craft not just effective teaching but also valuable learning opportunities that prepare students to thrive in real-life situations.

Essential Ideas to Remember

Intentional curriculum design starts with a clear grasp of the intended learning outcomes. Whether shaped by frameworks like Understanding by Design or Bloom's Taxonomy, it begins by specifying what students need to learn and be able to do. The resultant goals, outcomes, and objectives are then connected to assessments and activities. In AI-enhanced settings, this principle is especially vital; technology should support learning goals, not dictate them.

AI can be a powerful partner in designing goals, outcomes, and objectives when educators provide clear context, specify measurable verbs, and maintain alignment with overarching purposes. Well-designed prompts help AI tools generate relevant and actionable learning priorities, which educators can then refine for rigor, scope, and applicability. This collaboration frees up additional time for educators to spend engaging with students and fostering deeper learning experiences.

Clear, measurable goals and outcomes ensure that both human and AI contributions lead to authentic, transferable learning. Using Bloom's levels to select precise action verbs encourages outcomes that move beyond recall toward analysis, evaluation, and creation, cognitive domains where human insight is essential. In AI-integrated classrooms, this balance safeguards the distinct value of human judgment, creativity, and ethical reasoning.

Ultimately, purposeful learning design anchored in the WHY equips students to connect classroom experiences with real-world applications. By beginning with the end in mind, leveraging AI thoughtfully, and maintaining focus on meaningful outcomes, educators can create relevant learning journeys that are motivating and future focused.

References

Alaniz, K. (2021). *Collegial Coaching: Mentoring for Knowledge and Skills That Transfer to Real-World Applications*. Bloomsbury.

National Louis University (2024). *Using AI to Draft Learning Outcomes.* Learning Experience Design. https://nl.edu/lxd/ai-outcomes/.

Oregon State University (2024). *Advancing Meaningful Learning in the Age of AI.* Faculty Support. https://ecampus.oregonstate.edu/faculty/artificial-intelligence-tools/blooms-taxonomy-revisited/.

Pappas, C. (2024, April 25). *7 Ways to Enhance Learning Outcomes with the Help of AI.* eLearning Industry. https://elearningindustry.com/ways-to-enhance-learning-outcomes-with-the-help-of-ai.

Shabbir, R. (n.d.) *30 Examples of Bloom's Taxonomy Learning Objectives for Teachers.* Educationise. https://educationise.com/post/30-bloom-s-taxonomy-examples-of-learning-objectives-for-teachers/.

Sinek, S. (2011). *Start with Why.* Penguin.

Stanny, C.J. (2016). "Reevaluating Bloom's Taxonomy: What Measurable Verbs Can and Cannot Say About Student Learning." *Education Sciences*, 6(4): 37.

Stoeckle, A. (n.d.). *TILT 2.0-Worksheets for Students: Why Am I Doing This Assignment?* Wayne State University's Office for Teaching and Learning. https://docs.google.com/document/d/1ZmA6sO3JDHdrUH5MVGEMKuypD5uDVgrT/edit.

University of California Merced (2024). *Backwards Design: Start with Outcomes.* Teaching Commons. https://teach.ucmerced.edu/pedagogy-guides/backwards-design.

Wiggins, G. and J. McTighe (2011). *The Understanding by Design Guide to Creating High-Quality Units*. ASCD.

4 Assessment in the New World

Integrating Authentic Learning and AI in Everyday Educational Practice

"Life is a succession of lessons which must be lived to be understood."
HELEN KELLER

Historically, assessment has been treated as the final checkpoint, or a summative event that occurs after instruction, separate from the learning journey itself. Traditional tools like quizzes, tests, and written assignments tend to emphasize content recall and structured responses, often valuing efficiency over depth of understanding. In today's climate of heightened accountability, driven by standardized testing and stringent curriculum mandates, educators face the persistent challenge of balancing innovation with compliance. The time, freedom, and creative space required to design truly meaningful assessments are too often in short supply (Alaniz, 2021, 2024; Alaniz and Cerling, 2023).

However, the expanding presence of AI, and generative AI (GenAI) in particular, is reshaping what is possible in both instruction and assessment. AI tools can now provide real-time feedback, adaptive questioning, automated grading, and data-informed insights, allowing teachers to tailor assessments to individual learning needs. Rather than viewing assessments as static checkpoints, AI enables them to become dynamic and integrated aspects of the learning process, continuously adapting to student progress.

As described in Chapter 3, meaningful learning requires alignment between intended outcomes and assessment strategies. With AI integration, assessments can be personalized, interactive, and formative, guiding students throughout their educational journey rather than measuring learning only at the end.

Although education experts have long advocated for meaningful assessment, the integration of AI represents a pivotal opportunity to make this vision scalable and practical. Students who already engage with AI-enhanced tools are well-positioned to benefit from assessments that reflect their thinking, learning, and interaction with information. By embedding AI into instructional design and assessment practices, educators can foster deeper learning, support differentiation, and bridge the gap between instruction and evaluation in unprecedented ways.

AI integration has become a significant focus for educators across disciplines and academic levels. Rapid advancements in AI in recent years now enable students to easily generate coherent essays, presentations, images, videos, and other digital products by providing a prompt to a generative writing tool like ChatGPT (Keith, 2023).

As described by Keith (2023),

> *As the lion's share of popular and scholarly attention has fallen upon tools to generate written text, researchers and programmers in generative AI have branched out to other content areas, especially that of visual imagery. Tools now available to a wide audience include:*
>
> - *Midjourney, which can create customized images based upon a text prompt.*
> - *Tome, which generates entire slide decks with both text and images from a prompt.*
> - *Runway, a video creation tool.*
> - *Elicit, a "research aid" that, when given a research question, trawls existing scholarly work and extracts information it deems pertinent to that question.*
>
> *Even ChatGPT itself is being put to new applications beyond essay writing. Research suggests that it can fix bugs in computer code at least as well as, if not better than, existing machine learning models. (paras. 3–5)*

Naturally, the current versions of the tools mentioned above will soon become outdated and be replaced by more advanced AI tools capable of performing tasks that are not yet envisioned. On an academic level, deeper concerns include the risk of knowledge uniformity, threats to critical thinking, and the necessity to rethink how learning outcomes are assessed (Salinas-Navarro et al., 2024). To incorporate AI into education responsibly, it is crucial to prioritize human agency, ethical standards, and learner-centered approaches. This means aligning AI tools with students' needs, enhancing motivation, fostering interaction and higher-order thinking, and maintaining human oversight and accountability (Salinas-Navarro et al., 2024).

Research indicates that ChatGPT often exceeds the performance of the average student in many assessments, prompting a reconsideration of traditional evaluation practices in education (Geerling et al., 2023). Recommended adjustments include implementing authentic assessment measures and treating AI as a complement to, not a substitute for, student effort and engagement (Salinas-Navarro et al., 2024). Despite these concerns, AI tools offer educational benefits, including improving student writing, supporting personalized and adaptive learning, providing instant feedback, and serving as accessible learning aids, making them a valuable complement to human teaching when used responsibly and ethically (Salinas-Navarro et al., 2024).

As educators in the digital age strive to proactively, swiftly, and thoughtfully adapt to this new landscape, they position themselves and their students to ensure that assignment submissions reflect students' original ideas rather than those of AI tools. This helps learners move toward authentic learning, encouraging them to address essential goals, outcomes, and objectives.

In the words of Amoush and Farhat (2023),

> *Developing authentic assessment tasks might be the most effective approach for educators. Authentic tasks should be designed to represent what students do in their lives outside the educational institution and later when they graduate. This requires that they perform tasks intended for a real audience, and the student has an active role that simulates their role in life. Here, students are required to conduct an actual performance instead of simply providing an answer to a question or responding to a prompt. Such tasks require careful design that integrates collaboration among the learners, self and peer assessment, and presenting their outcomes in various formats. (para. 3)*

When educators create meaningful assessment strategies in advance, they often lessen the need for reactive measures, such as spending time identifying AI-generated work. An authentic approach to developing and implementing both formative and summative assessments, including rubrics to measure learning progress, empowers both educators and students to stay more effectively on track toward course goals, student learning outcomes, and lesson objectives.

The following chapter presents practical strategies for designing and implementing various assessment approaches, including those that intentionally incorporate AI, as well as those that offer learning opportunities beyond the use of AI. The chapter also includes questions to ponder and ideas to consider when designing both formative and summative assessments. Authentic assessment strategies can be integrated into any educational endeavor, with or without AI.

Purposeful Assessment in an AI-Enhanced Learning Environment

As discussed in earlier chapters, effective curriculum development and instructional design are rooted in the principles of beginning with the end in mind and identifying the purpose behind instruction. With the integration of AI, educators now have more powerful tools to design meaningful learning experiences that include clear criteria for assessing evidence of learning. AI-enhanced assessment platforms can help generate and evaluate authentic artifacts, such as multimedia projects, digital portfolios, or simulations, that more accurately reflect students' acquired knowledge and skills.

When educators introduce these assessment measures early and use AI to personalize and clarify expectations, students can better understand the rationale behind their learning journey and receive real-time feedback tailored to their progress. This proactive approach encourages reflection, motivation, and a deeper sense of purpose, inspiring learners to pursue meaningful goals. Students are most engaged when they see their learning as a bridge to their personal dreams and professional aspirations; without that connection, motivation can quickly fade. Authentic assessment, enhanced by AI, can help build that bridge by linking classroom learning to real-world applications through intelligent tutoring systems, career-focused simulations, and adaptive learning experiences.

An assessment is considered authentic when it involves directly evaluating students' performance on meaningful intellectual tasks. This approach is more applicable than using indirect, proxy, or overly simplified substitutes (Salinas-Navarro et al., 2024; Wiggins, 1990). Through authentic assessments, learners engage in realistic and purposeful activities, manage complexity, and tackle intellectual problems, enabling them to evaluate, make sense of, and progress toward mastery (Salinas-Navarro et al., 2024; Wiggins, 2011). All authentic assessments are performance-based because they require students to develop comprehensive responses, execute tasks, or create products effectively (Koh, 2017; Salinas-Navarro et al., 2024).

Authentic assessment is grounded in key principles of sound teaching design (Salinas-Navarro et al., 2024). It emphasizes applicability by presenting students with real-world or professional scenarios, paired with relevant and meaningful questions. These assessments are intellectually demanding, intended to foster advanced skills like applying knowledge, making decisions, and solving problems. They allow students to demonstrate understanding, activate prior knowledge, connect theory to practice, develop solutions, draw conclusions, and plan next steps (Salinas-Navarro et al., 2024).

A vital aspect of authentic assessment is the inclusion of evaluative judgment, where students learn to set standards and criteria to assess their own work, fostering self-directed and reflective learning (Salinas-Navarro et al., 2024). In essence, authentic assessment goes beyond traditional approaches by incorporating rich, varied, and engaging learning experiences. It uses multiple criteria to measure students' progress toward mastery and presents real-world, complex tasks. Unlike conventional assessments that often isolate skills, authentic assessments focus on identifying strengths and supporting growth rather than penalizing students (Salinas-Navarro et al., 2024).

As described by Wilson, Alaniz, and Sikora (2016),

> *In many cases, performance assessments provide more meaningful evaluations of learning for both teachers and students in determining*

strengths and weaknesses as related to instructional delivery and resultant student learning. These assessments combine measures of content area knowledge with opportunities to apply significant, real-world skills. Resultantly, they play a vital role in evaluating students' acquisition of twenty-first-century learning. (p. 117)

According to Wiggins (1998), an assessment opportunity is considered "authentic" when it reflects the complexities of real-life situations and meets criteria such as:

- The subject matter is represented in realistic and relevant ways.
- It requires students to apply judgment and innovation.
- Learners are actively engaged in solving meaningful problems.
- It mirrors professional or occupational tasks adults face.
- It evaluates the capacity to apply a variety of skills and understanding to solve difficult problems.
- It allows for practice, access to resources, feedback, and opportunities for revision.

In today's classrooms, AI-powered tools significantly expand the potential for authentic assessment. With AI integration, educators can create immersive environments, such as virtual labs and adaptive project-based tasks, that closely replicate professional scenarios in authentic and personalized ways. Students can engage with AI-driven platforms that prompt critical thinking, provide tailored feedback, and adapt in real-time to their progress.

When leveraged thoughtfully and purposefully, these technologies foster innovation, support creativity, and guide students through iterative learning processes, offering multiple opportunities for practice and refinement. For example, AI can offer suggestions, generate new challenges, or facilitate peer review cycles, making the assessment process more dynamic and reflective of how professionals learn and grow. Ultimately, AI-enhanced authentic assessments connect content knowledge with practical skill application in powerful, real-world ways. When paired with well-structured rubrics or digital scoring guides, AI tools help both educators and students stay aligned with learning goals throughout the planning, creation, and reflection phases.

Future-Oriented Instructional Design and Evaluation

The intersection of future-focused assessment design and technology integration is overviewed in *Collegial Coaching: Mentoring for Knowledge and Skills That Transfer to Real-world Applications* (Alaniz, 2021). However, this paradigm ultimately applies to any assessment experience:

> *Today's educators must remain mindful of the fact that they are preparing learners for jobs that might not even exist at this point. According to a report published by Dell Technologies and the Institute for the Future (2018), 85 percent of the jobs that will exist in 2030 have not even been invented yet. Although teachers in today's classrooms might not be able to predict what types of professions their students will pursue in the future, they can help them develop the skills they will need to successfully encounter any job opportunity—even those that have not yet been invented! Teachers in today's world are charged with the task of helping students dive into the DEEP end of learning experiences, supporting them as they* ***discover****,* ***engage****,* ***experiment****, and* ***produce****. (Alaniz, 2021, p. 94)*

Rather than relying solely on traditional assessment methods such as quizzes and exams, educators should design assessment strategies by first identifying the future-ready knowledge, skills, and competencies they want students to develop. This is especially important in light of the rapidly evolving digital and AI-enhanced world.

In today's fast-paced educational landscape, it is easy to become distracted by the appeal of the newest technological tools. Although innovation remains essential, an overemphasis on the most recent devices or flashy platforms can shift attention away from the more important goal of fostering transformational and lasting learning experiences. This is particularly relevant when integrating AI, not as a novelty, but as a purposeful enhancement to assessment and instruction.

Effective use of AI in assessment goes beyond automation or convenience. It involves utilizing AI to support personalized learning pathways, simulate real-world challenges, and deliver actionable insights that help students grow.

Instead of investing in short-lived technology, educators should prioritize instructional tools that align with long-term learning goals. These tools can empower students to develop critical thinking, adaptability, and digital fluency—skills they will need in the future.

> *Rather than focusing on using an interactive screen and having a device in every hand, teachers should be encouraged to provide opportunities for students to collaborate with classmates in solving real-world problems. Furthermore, they should facilitate experiences in which students create innovative products to share beyond the walls of their classroom... Impactful teaching in today's world focuses on making learning experiences authentic or more meaningful for students. When students are given opportunities to envision how they might use targeted knowledge and skills within a variety of future contexts, they will more naturally remain engaged and motivated throughout the learning process, ultimately making learning more memorable! (Alaniz, 2021, p. 94)*

Just as educators design lessons to support diverse learning goals, assessment formats should be intentionally developed to evaluate different dimensions of student learning. For example, assessments can be used to measure a student's prior knowledge or skill level, thereby confirming readiness for an upcoming unit or lesson. These are typically referred to as pre-assessments. Other assessments, conducted during instruction, help gauge student understanding and allow educators to modify their teaching strategies based on real-time student progress. These formative assessments play a crucial role in supporting instructional responsiveness. Summative assessments, by contrast, evaluate the level of learning achieved at the end of an instructional cycle (Alaniz, 2021; Alaniz, 2024; Alaniz and Cerling, 2023).

AI integration holds the potential to enhance how educators approach assessment, especially for those just beginning to utilize these tools. For instance, AI-powered systems can generate formative critical-thinking questions from lesson materials, analyze student responses, and identify concepts that need reteaching. They can also detect patterns in student work, such as recurring grammar mistakes in writing or repeated missteps in solving equations, before suggesting targeted follow-up activities. This approach makes formative assessment a continuous and adaptable process rather than a single checkpoint.

Summative assessments can also be improved through AI integration. For instance, AI tools can be leveraged to evaluate short-answer or essay responses and identify potential rubric mismatches for the teacher to review. They can also give students pre-submission feedback on clarity, structure, and use of evidence, allowing them to refine their work before the final deadline. In project-based learning, AI-assisted analysis of presentations can assess pacing, vocabulary choice, and alignment with rubric criteria, helping educators make their feedback more specific and meaningful. The data collected over time can assist educators in planning future units, addressing skill gaps, and monitoring student progress.

Because authentic assessments are grounded in real-world contexts, they can yield a wide range of results. The integration of artificial intelligence can enhance this process by suggesting ideas for and facilitating simulations, scenario-based assessments, or digital storytelling projects that mirror professional and practical challenges. Rubrics and digital scoring guides, discussed later in this chapter, help both educators and students stay aligned with the ultimate learning goals throughout the creation, reflection, and evaluation of each authentic learning artifact.

Authentic Approaches to Promoting Academic Integrity in the Age of AI

The growing presence of AI in education has introduced valuable opportunities, yet it also presents challenges to maintaining academic integrity (Raji, 2025). Traditional assessments are becoming more susceptible to misuse, as AI tools can produce convincing, human-like responses across a range of tasks. In contrast, authentic assessment offers a strong alternative by emphasizing real-world relevance, critical thinking, problem-solving, and the practical application of knowledge, areas that AI struggles to fully replicate (Forsyth and Evans, 2019).

Authentic assessment challenges students to apply their knowledge and skills in everyday contexts (McArthur, 2023; Raji, 2025), using approaches such as project-based learning, case studies, portfolios, and presentations. Raji (2025) overviews the benefits of using authentic assessment in an AI-driven world, including the following:

- **Fosters Deep Learning and Critical Thinking:** Authentic assessments encourage meaningful engagement with course content, promoting higher-order thinking. For example, students in a business course might create a marketing plan for an actual company, requiring them to conduct research, analyze data, and apply creative strategies, reducing dependence on responses produced by AI.
- **Limits Plagiarism and AI Misuse:** Because these assessments are typically tailored to specific situations and contexts, they are less likely to have pre-existing answers available online or through AI. A history assignment that involves producing a documentary on a local historical event, for instance, demands original research and personal interaction with the community, tasks that cannot easily be automated.
- **Promotes Collaboration and Communication:** Many authentic tasks involve teamwork and require effective communication skills that AI cannot replicate. In an engineering course, for example, students might work in groups to design and build a sustainable energy prototype. The hands-on, collaborative nature of the project ensures each student's contribution is distinct and verifiable.
- **Supports Ongoing Feedback and Reflection:** Authentic assessments often include opportunities for iterative feedback and self-reflection. In a creative writing class, students might maintain a portfolio of their work, revising pieces based on feedback from peers and instructors.

Authentic assessment endeavors allow students to actively reflect upon their learning, assess their progress, and understand how their knowledge and skills connect to the broader picture of their lives beyond the classroom. Amoush and Farhat (2023) outline the following strategies for optimizing authentic assessment in today's digital learning environments:

- Clarify the expectations for students from the outset of the task. Providing a written timeline and clear criteria communicates standards to students and gives them a defined focus for their efforts. These expectations delineate the extent and manner in which students should apply AI tools and necessitate acknowledgment of their use. This can be addressed for each assessment based on its unique requirements.

- Integrate a variety of assessment methods to establish a holistic, precise, and equitable evaluation system.
- Segment the task into manageable components to prevent students from feeling overwhelmed by receiving the entire task simultaneously.
- Throughout the work process, give constructive feedback to support students in staying on track and guide them toward the intended learning outcomes. This method offers students multiple chances to achieve their desired results, rather than restricting them to a single opportunity to meet the required standards. Align the task with the learning outcomes of the course, ensuring that students comprehend those connections.
- Provide students the opportunity to critique the work process and propose their own methodologies and guidelines.
- Educate students on the capabilities and limitations of artificial intelligence in their academic studies. It may be beneficial to present examples illustrating how AI can sometimes yield biased or inaccurate information.
- Clearly outline the permissible uses of AI in the classroom, specifying what is acceptable for assignments and what is prohibited.
- Most importantly, maintain an ongoing dialogue with students to understand their perceptions and experiences, while sharing personal and professional insights. Use ethics as a guiding principle in these conversations to help them make informed decisions when using these tools.

Additionally, educators can implement measures at the individual assessment level to decrease the chances of AI-facilitated academic dishonesty. Keith (2023) recommends the following strategies:

- ***Promote close reading with Hypothesis.*** *Hypothesis, a digital tool for collaborative annotation, is designed to help students drill down into a text. It also promotes the collective construction of knowledge, as students respond to each other's annotations and ask questions that can further discourse. Not only can the use of Hypothesis make reading a more engaging activity, but it also builds the vital skill of extracting information from a text. This may help to make your students less dependent on Elicit and similar tools that (purport to) do the heavy lifting of information-gathering for them.*

- ***Teach students citation management.*** *EndNote and Zotero are two UChicago-supported tools for managing citations. Unlike Elicit, however, they rely on the student's own judgment to decide what material is worth citing. As part of a more general program, wherein you explain to your students not only* ***how*** *to cite, but also* ***why*** *citation is vital, these tools can help them to do the intellectual spadework of building a bibliography without being dependent on AI . . .*
- ***Assign students to create a podcast.*** *Podcasting assignments are an excellent way to help students express themselves meaningfully. What's more, it is much more difficult to fake a podcast with AI—particularly if it happens to be in interview format—than to generate an image or a video. With a personalized assessment (e.g., "Talk about your experiences growing up in X country"), students will be both less* ***inclined*** *to cheat and less* ***able*** *to cheat. (paras. 15, 16, 18)*

Raji (2025) shares the following examples and strategies for implementing authentic assessments that encourage meaningful learning while adhering to academic integrity principles:

Service-Learning Projects

- **Strategy:** Service-learning involves students collaborating with community partners to address real-world challenges while applying classroom knowledge. These experiences are highly individualized and context-specific, making them difficult to replicate with AI-generated content.
- **Example:** Assign students to work with local non-profit organizations to identify a community issue, design a response plan, and implement a solution. Students then submit a reflective report documenting their actions, decisions, and learning outcomes.

Capstone Projects

- **Strategy:** Capstone projects require students to synthesize knowledge from across their coursework in a culminating, hands-on project. These tasks involve multiple phases, such as design, testing, and revision, highlighting student growth and original work.

- **Example:** Final-year students might be asked to design, construct, and evaluate a prototype relevant to their field. They present their work to a panel of industry professionals and incorporate feedback into their final deliverable.

Role-Playing Simulations

- **Strategy:** Simulations place students in complex, real-life roles that require research, decision-making, and collaboration. Because each student's approach and response are unique, these activities reduce reliance on AI-generated input.
- **Example:** Students might take on professional roles (e.g., policy advisor, healthcare worker, entrepreneur) in a simulated scenario. They research their role, prepare a position or plan, and interact with others in character to demonstrate understanding of key concepts.

Reflective Journals

- **Strategy:** Reflective journals help students connect course content with their personal learning experiences. The introspective and evolving nature of these entries makes them inherently original and difficult to outsource to AI.
- **Example:** Ask students to maintain a reflective journal throughout the term, where they document their reactions to course materials, insights from class discussions, and personal growth.

Peer Review and Feedback

- **Strategy:** Peer review builds critical thinking and analytical skills by encouraging students to assess and improve each other's work. This collaborative process promotes originality and discourages the use of AI-generated submissions.
- **Example:** Incorporate peer review sessions where students exchange drafts and offer feedback. Require revisions based on peer input to help students strengthen their work through reflection and iteration.

Rubrics to Guide Authentic Learning Experiences

Evaluating authentic learning experiences differs from grading traditional assessments like quizzes or exams. Educators must determine how well the final product demonstrates the intended knowledge and skills when creating authentic assessments and reviewing students' learning artifacts.

In the words of Wilson, Alaniz, and Sikora (2016),

> *Skillfully designed criteria-based rubrics enable students to apprehend specifically how their work will be evaluated, even before they begin the project. This way, students—and not just their teachers—receive the opportunity to "begin with the end in mind," focusing more specifically and purposefully on meeting predetermined criteria for excellence, rather than blindly and haphazardly piecing together their project. Rubrics may support teachers in alleviating "surprise" elements of grading, as students gain insights regarding how the grading process will unfold. With the use of rubrics, issues may arise when students—especially those who are operating at higher levels—begin to "aim low," just barely meeting the requirements outlined in the rubric rather than striving for excellence. These situations may be avoided by adding features to the rubric to encourage students to reach their fullest potential through unconventional methods. "Creativity points" or points for "going above and beyond" in unique ways might encourage additional innovation from learners. (p. 119)*

An effective rubric establishes distinct performance expectations while offering students specific feedback (Nolen, 2024). It includes three main components: evaluation criteria, a scoring scale, and quality descriptions for each criterion. The latter element is what complicates rubric design. The criteria specify which aspects of a task will be evaluated, and the scoring scale measures the level of performance quality; however, it is the descriptors that enable learners to effectively evaluate their own work and plan targeted improvements (Nolen, 2024).

In the era of AI-assisted learning, rubrics are more essential than ever, not only as tools for assessment but as frameworks for fostering academic integrity, critical thinking, and meaningful collaboration. Rubrics offer a structured approach for encouraging peer review prior to final submission, supporting students in developing key skills such as giving and receiving feedback, posing thoughtful questions, and offering constructive critiques. This process enables both reviewers and reviewees to engage in a deeper analysis of their work, thereby enhancing focus, accountability, and mutual learning (Alaniz, 2021; Alaniz, 2024; Alaniz and Cerling, 2023; Wilson, Alaniz, and Sikora, 2016).

Importantly, rubrics also function as a form of AI-resistant pedagogy. When well-crafted criteria guide students, they are more likely to engage with the learning process and less likely to rely on generative AI to shortcut their efforts. Rubrics help demystify the expectations behind an assignment, making learning goals transparent and accessible. Such transparency supports student comprehension while fostering open communication between teachers and students about what success entails and how it can be attained.

Effective rubric design in this context must be responsive to both instructional goals and the realities of AI in education. Rubrics should be discipline-specific, developmentally appropriate, and tailored to the objectives of each unit or assignment. Moreover, teaching students how to interpret, reflect on, and apply rubric feedback equips them to exercise agency over their learning experiences. This metacognitive engagement further discourages overreliance on AI and instead cultivates deeper learning and ethical academic practices.

As described by Keith (2023),

> *Rubrics are assignment-specific and can be used to lay out the criteria by which a submission will be graded, so that students can better understand what you are looking for: are the mechanics of writing foremost, for example, or is originality of thought more important? Outcomes, meanwhile, can be connected to multiple assessments… making it possible both for you to track students' progress across the various competencies and for them to see that the work you are assigning has a purpose. As with AI tools, so in general, highly motivated students are less likely to resort to dishonest methods. (para. 13)*

The rubrics below are adapted from those initially found in *Digital Media in Today's Classrooms: The Potential for Meaningful Teaching, Learning, and Assessment* (Wilson, Alaniz, and Sikora, 2016).

Sample Digital Media Rubric for Assessment of a Project Created by an Individual Student:

Project Title: "Life Cycles in Nature"
Digital Tool Used: iMovie, Book Creator, or Other Digital Storytelling Tool

Criteria Topic	**"Excellent" Criteria 10 points**	**"Acceptable" Criteria 7 points**	**"Poor" Criteria 4 Points**
Pictures	Pictures are clear and give excellent added meaning to the life cycle process illustrated.	Pictures are mostly clear and give some added meaning to the life cycle process illustrated.	Some pictures are not clear and distract the viewer from learning the life cycle process.
Narration	Narrator does an excellent job describing at least three different life cycles.	Narrator does an acceptable job describing at least three different life cycles (or an excellent job describing just two examples).	Narrator does not illustrate the different stages of life cycles.
Music	Music effectively correlates with the content of the project and enhances the quality of the presentation.	Music seems an acceptable choice considering the content of the presentation.	Music does not seem to fit the content of the presentation.
Video Segments	Video segments effectively correlate with the content of the project and enhance the quality of the presentation.	Video segments seem an acceptable choice considering the content of the presentation.	Video segments do not seem to fit the content of the presentation.

Criteria Topic	"Excellent" Criteria 10 points	"Acceptable" Criteria 7 points	"Poor" Criteria 4 Points
Text	Text effectively correlates with the content of the project and enhances the quality of the presentation.	Text seems an acceptable choice considering the content of the presentation.	Text does not seem to fit the content of the presentation.
Font and Style	Font and style effectively correlate with the content of the project and enhances the quality of the presentation.	Font and style seem an acceptable choice considering the content of the presentation.	Font and style do not seem to fit the content of the presentation.
Creativity	Highly creative methods of describing the different types of life cycles are evident throughout the presentation.	Some creative methods are evident throughout the presentation.	Creative methods are not evident throughout the presentation. The individual did not incorporate creativity beyond what was expected.
Citations and References	The presentation includes citations and references for all resources used.	The presentation includes citations and references for most resources used.	The presentation includes few to no citations and references for resources used.

Educators can use rubrics tailored to specific tasks, assignments, or both to evaluate collaborative projects with various student roles and outcomes. When a project requires students to collaborate on every part, a rubric emphasizing participation or teamwork is more appropriate. The following rubrics can provide valuable insights into each student's contributions toward the project's overall goals and results.

Group Member Completing the Form: Sample Group Member 4
Group Participation Rubric
Group Member 1:

Criteria Topic	**"Excellent" Criteria 10 points**	**"Acceptable" Criteria 7 points**	**"Poor" Criteria 4 Points**
Completed daily assignments on time. (Contributions)	Group member 1 always completed homework and assignments on time.	Group member 1 usually completed homework and assignments on time.	Group member 1 was often late on completing assigned work.
Worked well with others. (Attitude)	Group member 1 always worked well with the group.	Group member 1 usually worked well with the group.	Group member 1 didn't work well with the group.
Helped others on their assignments. (Teamwork)	Group member 1 helped me with my assignment.	Group member 1 didn't help me but didn't distract me on my assignment.	Group member 1 didn't help me and distracted me while working on my group assignment.
Stayed on task during class. (Effectiveness)	Group member 1 always did what the teacher expected in class.	Group member 1 did what the teacher expected in class.	Group member 1 caused distractions in class.

Group Member Completing the Form: Sample Group Member 4
Group Participation Rubric
Group Member 2: ____________________

Criteria Topic	**Criteria Topic**	**Criteria Topic**	**Criteria Topic**
Completed daily assignments on time. (Contributions)	Group member 2 always completed homework and assignments on time.	Group member 2 usually completed homework and assignments on time.	Group member 2 was often late on completing assigned work.
Worked well with others. (Attitude)	Group member 2 always worked well with the group.	Group member 2 usually worked well with the group.	Group member 2 didn't work well with the group.

Criteria Topic	Criteria Topic	Criteria Topic	Criteria Topic
Helped others on their assignments. (Teamwork)	Group member 2 helped me with my assignment.	Group member 2 didn't help me but didn't distract me on my assignment.	Group member 2 didn't help me and distracted me while working on my group assignment.
Stayed on task during class. (Effectiveness)	Group member 2 always did what the teacher expected in class.	Group member 2 did what the teacher expected in class.	Group member 2 caused distractions in class.

Group Member Completing the Form: Sample Group Member 4

Group Participation Rubric

Group Member 3: ____________________

Criteria Topic	Criteria Topic	Criteria Topic	Criteria Topic
Completed daily assignments on time. (Contributions)	Group member 3 always completed homework and assignments on time.	Group member 3 usually completed homework and assignments on time.	Group member 3 was often late on completing assigned work.
Worked well with others. (Attitude)	Group member 3 always worked well with the group.	Group member 3 usually worked well with the group.	Group member 3 didn't work well with the group.
Helped others on their assignments. (Teamwork)	Group member 3 helped me with my assignment.	Group member 3 didn't help me but didn't distract me on my assignment.	Group member 3 didn't help me and distracted me while working on my group assignment.
Stayed on task during class. (Effectiveness)	Group member 3 always did what the teacher expected in class.	Group member 3 did what the teacher expected in class.	Group member 3 caused distractions in class.

Many educational websites showcase ready-made rubrics that effectively address a variety of student learning outcomes. For educators wanting to create original rubrics, numerous websites specifically support this goal. Rubistar (http://rubistar.4teachers.org) is an excellent tool that empowers teachers to design their own rubrics without starting from scratch. This platform provides several templates that allow educators to input predefined criteria and modify them according to the specific course goals, student learning outcomes, and learning objectives pertinent to various assessments.

TeAch-nology (http://www.teach-nology.com/web_tools/rubrics/) offers resources for the development of customizable rubrics and gives educators access to an extensive collection of pre-existing rubrics. Furthermore, the platform provides materials aimed at enhancing student engagement in authentic assessment activities, particularly those that incorporate digital tools and resources. Additionally, it features complimentary tutorials intended to aid in the creation of digital assessment products.

Figure 4.1 Rubistar QR Code.

The Faculty Innovation Center at the University of Texas at Austin provides a valuable resource (https://ctl.utexas.edu/sites/default/files/build-rubric.pdf) to support educators in exploring the following questions:

Figure 4.2 TeAchnology QR Code.

- What is a rubric?
- What does a rubric look like?
- Where do I start the process of creating a rubric?
- How can I design a rubric?
- What can I consider as I review a rubric?
- Where can I learn more?

In addition to utilizing the tools described above, educators can enhance the efficiency of the rubric creation process by leveraging AI tools (Nolen, 2024). To begin, it is essential to formulate an AI prompt that clearly delineates the requirements for the assignment. This prompt should

Figure 4.3 The University of Texas at Austin Faculty Innovation Center Rubric Guide QR Code.

encompass the assignment or task, course objectives, scoring scale, desired criteria, and instruction for evaluation descriptors.

Nolen (2024) offers the example below, featuring the creation of a rubric associated with a problem designed to assess students' understanding of Newton's Laws of Motion:

> *Task: The values of masses m1 and m2 are 2 kg and 3 kg, respectively, in the system shown in the attached image. The friction coefficient between the inclined plane and mass m1 is 0.5. If the system is released, find the values of acceleration and tension in the string. (sin37 = 0.6, cos37 = 0.8, g = 10 m/s^2)*
>
> *Prompt Engineering: To create an effective prompt, we first need to tell the AI platform what we want it to do. In this case, we want it to design a rubric. We can say: "Create a well-crafted and clear rubric for students in the form of a table using student-friendly language."*
>
> *Next, we need to include the assignment description by simply copying and pasting the instructions. For tasks that include an image, like our physics example above, have the image available as a separate file to upload into the generative AI platform. If the generative AI platform cannot read or interpret pictures or images, then write a detailed description of the image.*
>
> *At the time this article was published, Copilot was able to interpret images while the free version of ChatGPT (3.5) was not. We can say:*
>
> *The rubric is for the following student task description: The values of masses m1 and m2 are 2 kg and 3 kg, respectively, in the system shown in the attached image. The friction coefficient between the inclined plane and mass m1 is 0.5. If the system is released, find the values of acceleration and tension in the string. (sin37 = 0.6, cos37 = 0.8, g = 10 m/s^2)*
>
> *The language and terminology used in rubrics should align with course objectives, which means we should also include the course learning objectives in our prompt. For our physics example, we can say:*
>
> *The rubric should be aligned with the following course learning objectives: Upon successfully completing this course, you will have come to understand the basic principles governing the motion of objects, learned to think more critically/scientifically, and developed the skills needed to attack difficult*

problems. These are all skills that will serve you strongly in your future courses and careers, even if you never again consider a block sliding down an incline.

Next, we need to tell the AI platform what type of rubric we would like to create. This includes the three essential parts of a rubric. For our physics example, we can say: "The rubric should contain three parts: Scoring and Scale, Criteria, and Descriptors. Use the following scoring scale for the rubric:

- *Exemplary (4 points)*
- *Proficient (3 points)*
- *Basic (2 points)*
- *Beginning (1 point)*

Include the following criteria for each element of the scoring scale I just mentioned above:

- *Axes*
- *Drawing free-body diagrams*
- *Representation of forces*
- *Type and direction of motion*
- *Solutions for equations*
- *Units"*

Next, we need to provide a clear description of the type of descriptors we need for each criteria. This is often the most difficult and time-intensive part of rubric creation, but AI can quickly do this task in student-friendly language. Continuing with our example, we can say:

For each of the criteria and each scoring scale, generate a descriptor that focuses on describing the quality of the work rather than simply the quantity. Emphasize what constitutes exemplary, proficient, basic, and beginning performance in terms of meeting the objectives of the task, rather than just the quantity of work produced. For example, descriptors should highlight the depth of understanding, clarity of communication, accuracy of information, relevance to the topic, adherence to conventions, and effectiveness of practical implications, among other qualitative aspects.

Finally, we need to tell the AI platform what rubric form we would like. The most common form is a table. We can say:

Generate the rubric in the form of a table. The first row heading for the table should include the scoring scale and points. The first column on the left of the table should display the criteria. The descriptors for each component and score should be listed under the correct scoring scale and points column and criteria row. Make the descriptors in the table as specific to the objectives as possible.

When we put all of this together into one prompt, we generated the following rubric. (paras. 4–10). Please see the resulting rubric on pages 84 and 85.

From this point, the educator can modify the rubric or adjust the prompt as needed. Instead of creating a new rubric from scratch for every assignment, they may choose to apply a framework such as Nolen's (2024), allowing AI to handle the initial rubric design based on specific prompts.

Whether achieved with or without the assistance of AI, rubric development plays a vital role in authentic assessment initiatives. Rubrics not only furnish a clear framework for evaluation but also enhance transparency, consistency, and fairness within the assessment process, ensuring that learners comprehend the expectations and criteria that will guide their performance. This systematic approach enables educators to evaluate student work efficiently, fostering an environment in which feedback is meaningful and supports student engagement, motivation, and growth.

Implementation Challenges in Applying Authentic Assessment with AI Integration

Although authentic assessment offers numerous benefits for both learners and educators, it is crucial to acknowledge the real-world challenges encountered when implementing these strategies, particularly when reconciling traditional expectations with the integration of modern technologies, such as AI. For example, designing authentic assessments requires more time and planning compared to traditional tests. Tasks such as creating rubrics, managing collaborative projects, and providing personalized feedback are labor-intensive and time-consuming. This can be especially difficult for educators who manage large classes or teach multiple subjects.

Resulting Rubric

Criteria	Exemplary (4 points)	Proficient (3 points)	Basic (2 points)	Below Basic (1 point)
Axes	Axes are correctly labeled with appropriate scales and units, enhancing the clarity and accuracy of the solution.	Axes are labeled and have scales, but may lack precision or have minor errors.	Axes are present but lack labels or scales, leading to some confusion.	Axes are either not present or incorrectly drawn, severely impacting the clarity of the solution.
Drawing free-body diagrams	Diagrams are meticulously drawn with all forces accurately represented; they enhance understanding of the system's motion.	Diagrams include most forces and are fairly accurate but may lack some detail or precision.	Diagrams include essential forces but lack accuracy or detail, offering limited aid in understanding the system's motion.	Diagrams are either missing or inaccurately drawn, offering no aid in understanding the system's motion.
Representation of forces	Forces are represented with high precision; arrows' sizes and directions perfectly depict force magnitudes and directions contributing to a deeper understanding of the problem.	Forces are mostly accurate; minor errors in size or direction do not significantly impede understanding.	Force representation lacks precision in size or direction, leading to potential misunderstandings of their effects.	Forces are either not represented or done so inaccurately that it obstructs problem-solving processes.

Criteria	Exemplary (4 points)	Proficient (3 points)	Basic (2 points)	Below Basic (1 point)
Type and direction of motion	The type and direction of motion is analyzed with exceptional clarity; insights into their implications on equations and solutions is evident, enhancing critical thinking skills.	The type and direction is identified correctly but lacks depth in analysis, affecting critical thinking development slightly.	Type and direction is mentioned but not analyzed deeply enough to foster a strong development of critical thinking skills.	The type and direction is either incorrect or not mentioned at all, hindering development of critical thinking skills entirely.
Solutions for equations	Solutions demonstrate an exceptional grasp over principles governing objects' motions; they're accurate, detailed, promoting a robust scientific thought process.	Solutions show a good grasp over principles but may contain minor errors that don't majorly impact comprehension.	Solutions indicate basic understanding but contain significant errors reflecting gaps in knowledge acquisition.	Solutions reflect a poor grasp over principles containing fundamental errors obstructing the learning process.
Units	Units are consistently correct and appropriately used throughout the solution, demonstrating a strong understanding of the problem.	Units are mostly correct but may have minor inconsistencies or errors.	Units are used but contain significant errors or inconsistencies, indicating a lack of understanding.	Units are either not used or used incorrectly, severely hindering the understanding of the problem.

Source: Nolen, 2024.

Furthermore, many educators have not received formal training in authentic assessment methodologies or in meaningfully integrating AI within learning environments. Consequently, they may experience uncertainty regarding the design of assignments that encourage students to utilize the tools of the age, such as AI, in meaningful and ethical ways. Professional development initiatives and collegial coaching practices are crucial to bridging this gap (Alaniz, 2021; Alaniz and Wilson, 2015).

Additionally, in the contemporary educational landscape, an emphasis on high-stakes testing and inflexible pacing guides can restrict teachers' autonomy to experiment with authentic assessment strategies. Within systems where accountability is linked to standardized metrics, educators may feel compelled to prioritize "teaching to the test" over pedagogical innovation. Moreover, integrating AI tools into learning can hinder fair participation due to differences in device availability, internet access, and software skills. Educators must ensure that AI-based assessments do not inadvertently increase achievement gaps.

In addition to structural and logistical issues, educators should consider how various educational environments impact the design and execution of authentic assessments. In schools with limited access to AI tools or reliable internet, teachers can emphasize community-based projects, experiential learning, or oral storytelling (Alaniz, 2024). These low-tech or no-tech methods continue to promote critical thinking, teamwork, and creativity, while encouraging deeper learning. In special education, authentic assessments offer students opportunities to showcase their grasp of content in ways that accommodate their diverse abilities and needs. These might include visual portfolios, hands-on models, or audio journals tailored to each student's strengths.

Adult and alternative education learners also benefit from assessments linked to workforce skills and practical life competencies. Tasks such as designing resumes, developing business plans, or proposing civic initiatives provide immediate relevance. Furthermore, culturally responsive assessment approaches that reflect students' identities, languages, and experiences foster more meaningful engagement and purposeful learning.

Standards Alignment and Accreditation Considerations

While authentic assessment may appear to conflict with standardized evaluation frameworks, an increasing body of research and policy guidance affirms that these methodologies can, in fact, be harmonized with the stipulated standards and accreditation criteria. By implementing the backward design model, initiating with standards and desired outcomes, educators can ensure that performance tasks and projects directly correspond to established benchmarks (Wiggins and McTighe, 2005).

Carefully developed rubrics can then convert these benchmarks into measurable and meaningful criteria. Educational institutions and districts can further facilitate this alignment by creating standards that explicitly demonstrate how authentic assessments address specific indicators on state examinations or accreditation frameworks. For instance, a capstone project might satisfy both writing standards and career readiness competencies.

In higher education, accreditation agencies are increasingly endorsing competency-based measures such as portfolios, capstones, and reflective journals as legitimate evidence of learning and skill acquisition (McArthur, 2023). These assessment tools provide robust alternatives to traditional examinations, while meeting institutional and program-level requirements. Importantly, authentic assessments do not entirely replace standardized measures; rather, they provide vital scaffolding that fosters transferable skills, such as analysis, synthesis, and reasoning, supporting students in succeeding on more conventional assessments as well.

Future-Thinking and Co-Design in Education

Looking ahead, authentic assessment not only provides practical answers to current educational needs but also paves the way for more innovative, student-centered, and future-oriented methods of learning and evaluation. This human-centered approach encourages educators to empathize with students' needs, define problems, generate creative ideas, prototype learning activities, and refine them through feedback. When students actively participate in designing assessments, their sense of ownership and engagement increases. Co-creating tasks enables learners to help set evaluation criteria, choose suitable formats, or suggest real-world problems to solve, fostering intrinsic motivation.

As technology continues to advance, AI literacy is no longer optional; it is a critical learning goal. If students are not taught to use AI meaningfully and ethically during their schooling years, they risk falling behind as they enter professional environments where AI competence will be an expectation rather than an advantage. Integrating opportunities to work with AI in assessments, such as evaluating the accuracy and bias of AI-generated content, crafting precise prompts, or reflecting on human-AI collaboration, ensures students gain both the technical skill and ethical grounding to use these tools responsibly. In this way, authentic assessment not only meets today's educational standards but also prepares students to thrive in a future where AI fluency is essential for success.

Essential Ideas to Remember

Traditional assessments often concentrate on evaluating student learning after instruction. Alternatively, integrating assessment into the learning process encourages deeper engagement, supports reflection, and empowers students to attain key academic objectives. Authentic assessment aligns learning with real-world application, inspiring students to actively engage with content, think critically, and demonstrate their understanding through complex, performance-based tasks rather than mere recall.

As AI tools continue to advance, educators must ensure that assessment practices genuinely reflect students' original thinking and skill development. When designed with deliberate intent and clarity, authentic assessments can diminish academic dishonesty, promote ethical technology use, and cultivate more meaningful learning experiences. Clearly articulated learning outcomes are foundational to such endeavors. By designing assessments that embody these outcomes and simulate real-world challenges, educators can maintain student engagement and accountability.

Utilizing a combination of authentic pre-assessments, formative assessments, and summative assessments provides a comprehensive and continuous perspective on student learning. This approach allows for timely feedback, instructional adjustments, and student self-directed learning. Well-crafted rubrics further support this process by clarifying expectations, facilitating self-assessment, and ensuring fair and transparent grading. They also encourage peer review and collaboration, inspiring students to take ownership of their work and learning journey.

Today's educators bear the responsibility of preparing students for careers that may yet be undefined. Through intentional assessment design, they can cultivate essential skills such as creativity, collaboration, adaptability, and ethical decision-making. By explicitly articulating the purpose and proper application of AI within academic settings, educators assist students in developing digital literacy and responsible practices. Open discussions about AI's capabilities and limitations, rooted in ethics and transparency, foster a culture of integrity and reflection.

Ultimately, authentic assessment is more than an instructional strategy; it represents a transformative approach to teaching and learning. It invites educators to craft learning experiences that are relevant, rigorous, and relational. Such experiences prepare students not only to meet contemporary academic standards but also to excel in a rapidly evolving world. When students perceive their learning as purposeful, interconnected, and future-oriented, they are significantly more motivated, curious, and engaged. As they adopt authentic assessment approaches, educators embrace their role as architects of meaningful, enduring learning experiences.

References

Alaniz, K. (2021). *Collegial Coaching: Mentoring for Knowledge and Skills That Transfer to Real-World Applications*. Rowman & Littlefield.

Alaniz, K. (2024). *A Learning Community Built on Strengths: Inspiring Educators to Positively Impact Student Lives*. Bloomsbury.

Alaniz, K. and D. Wilson (2015). *Naturalizing Digital Immigrants: The Power of Collegial Coaching for Technology Integration*. Bloomsbury.

Alaniz, K. and K. Cerling (2023). *Authentic Assessment in Action: An Everyday Guide for Bringing Learning to Life Through Meaningful Assessment*. Bloomsbury.

Amoush, S.A. and A. Farhat (2023, December 13). "The Power of Authentic Assessment in the Age of AI." *Faculty Focus*. https://www.facultyfocus.com/articles/educational-assessment/the-power-of-authentic-assessment-in-the-age-of-ai/.

Forsyth, H. and J. Evans (2019). "Authentic Assessment for a More Inclusive History." *Higher Education Research and Development*, 38(4): 748–61.

Geerling, W., G.D. Mateer, J. Wooten, and N. Damodaran (2023). "ChatGPT Has Aced the Test of Understanding in College Economics: Now What?" *American Economist*, 68(2): 233–45.

Institute for the Future (IFTF), for Dell Technologies. (2018). *Realizing 2030: A Divided Vision of the Future: Global Business Leaders Forecast the Next Era of Human-Machine Partnerships and How They Intend to Prepare* [summary]. Retrieved from https://www.delltechnologies.com/content/dam/delltechnologies/assets/perspectives/2030/pdf/Realizing-2030-A-Divided-Vision-of-the-Future-Summary.pdf.

Keith, T. (2023, February 7). *Combating Academic Dishonesty, Part 7: Authentic Assessments and the Challenge of AI*. The University of Chicago: Academic Technology Solutions. https://academictech.uchicago.edu/2023/02/07/combating-academic-dishonesty-part-7-authentic-assessments-and-the-challenge-of-ai/.

Koh, K.H. (2017). "Authentic Assessment." In *Oxford Research Encyclopedia of Education*. Oxford University Press. Available online: https://oxfordre.com/education/search?q0=Authentic+Assessment.

McArthur, J. (2023). "Rethinking Authentic Assessment: Work, Well-Being, and Society." *Higher Education*, 85: 85–101. https://doi.org/10.1007/s10734-022-00822-y.

Nolen, A. (2024, May 1). *Unlocking Academic Excellence: Using Generative AI to Create Custom Rubrics*. Center for Teaching and Learning. https://blog.ctl.gatech.edu/2024/05/01/unlocking-academic-excellence-using-generative-ai-to-create-custom-rubrics/.

Raji, M. (2025, March 25). *Smart Solutions: Authentic Assessment for AI-era Academic Integrity*. Teaching and Learning, Conestoga College. https://tlconestoga.ca/smart-solutions-authentic-assessment-for-AI-era-academic-integrity.

Salinas-Navarro, D.E., E. Vilalta-Perdomo, R. Michel-Villarreal, and L. Montesinos (2024). "Using Generative Artificial Intelligence Tools to Explain and Enhance Experiential Learning for Authentic Assessment." *Education Sciences*, 14(1): 83.

Wiggins, G. (1990). "The Case for Authentic Assessment." *Practical Assessment, Research, and Evaluation*, 2(1): 1–3.

Wiggins, G. (1998). "Ensuring Authentic Performance." In *Educative Assessment: Designing Assessments to Inform and Improve Student Performance* (pp. 21–42). Jossey-Bass.

Wiggins, G. (2011). "A True Test: Toward More Authentic and Equitable Assessment." *Phi Delta Kappan*, 92(7): 81–93.
Wiggins, G.P. and J. McTighe (2005). *Understanding by Design*. ASCD.
Wilson, D., K. Alaniz, and J. Sikora (2016). *Digital Media in Today's Classrooms: The Potential for Meaningful Teaching, Learning, and Assessment*. Bloomsbury.

5 The Authentic Learning Framework

Engaging with Everyday Issues, Real-world Audiences, and Meaningful Assessment

"The world is becoming more complex, uncertain, and fast-moving, and students need to become problem solvers, communicators, and change-makers."
MICHAEL FULLAN

The rapid pace of digital innovation constantly challenges educators and students to adapt, rethink, and reimagine how learning occurs. This is especially clear in the rapidly changing field of artificial intelligence. Since the launch of ChatGPT in November 2022, followed by numerous other AI chatbots, discussions about AI have filled campuses, conferences, and professional forums. One of the most important topics in this ongoing conversation is how to use AI, particularly generative AI (GenAI), to enhance student learning through its thoughtful integration into authentic assessment (Dolbin et al., 2024).

This strategy offers several advantages: it equips students with the digital literacy skills necessary for their future careers, fosters engagement with AI while encouraging learners to assess AI-generated materials critically, and ultimately enhances their critical thinking abilities. Additionally, if appropriately structured, it can guide students to tackle complex problems with a more comprehensive perspective. Adapting assessments in this manner may also alleviate some concerns faculty members have regarding academic integrity, particularly with students using AI with increasing regularity to complete assignments (Dolbin et al., 2024).

When educators design and implement authentic learning experiences, especially those powered by AI, students gain memorable and impactful moments that transcend the traditional classroom. The most successful educators recognize that AI can personalize and contextualize learning in ways that ignite intrinsic motivation, especially when learning aligns with real-life situations and future-facing technologies. AI-enhanced authentic learning opportunities can radically shift educational practices, empowering students to move from passive recipients of information to active co-creators in meaningful learning experiences.

A framework for authentic learning is presented in the book *Collegial Coaching: Mentoring for Knowledge and Skills That Transfer to Real-World Applications* (Alaniz, 2021); educators promote meaningful learning endeavors through implementing thoughtful instructional strategies based on applicability:

> *They do this by offering [students] real-world problems to solve, giving them opportunities to present solutions to various audiences, and designing assessment endeavors that apply to the everyday lives of learners. This method is summed up in an innovative formula for meaningful learning: authentic issues + authentic audiences + authentic assessment = authentic learning experiences. (p. 92)*

In AI-infused classrooms, this formula is further enhanced. AI tools can help educators identify authentic issues relevant to students' interests and local or global challenges. They can also simulate real-world audiences through virtual reality, chatbots, and feedback systems. Even assessments can be dynamically generated or tailored by AI to reflect real-life applications. Yet, even with AI, the foundation remains: educators must begin with the end in mind and clearly communicate the WHY behind learning.

Educators without a clear purpose in their planning and execution will likely struggle to inspire a genuine passion for learning in their students. When educators present learning outcomes and assessments to students, it is crucial to keep purpose at the forefront. This approach fosters intrinsic motivation, helps students persist through academic challenges, and ultimately leads to their success in achieving learning outcomes (Alaniz, 2021; Alaniz, 2024; Alaniz and Cerling, 2023).

Purpose is achieved by connecting learning activities to real life, something AI can make more accessible by analyzing student data and customizing content. When students see how AI-assisted tools or simulations mirror future careers or personal challenges, engagement increases. AI does not replace real-world experience but enriches the process by enabling students to test scenarios, receive instant feedback, and iterate in safe, dynamic environments. Although educators may not be able to predict the specific career paths students will follow, AI can help guide students in developing essential, transferable skills for any professional future.

The previously mentioned white paper by Fullan and Scott (2014) emphasizes innovative instructional strategies aimed at future-oriented education learning:

- ***Character:*** *"Qualities of the individual essential for being personally effective in a complex world, including grit, tenacity, perseverance, resilience, reliability, and honesty."*
- ***Citizenship:*** *"Thinking like global citizens, considering global issues based on a deep understanding of diverse values with genuine interest in engaging with others to solve complex problems that impact human and environmental sustainability."*
- ***Collaboration:*** *"The capacity to work interdependently and synergistically in teams with strong interpersonal and team-related skills including effective management of team dynamics, making substantive decisions together, and learning from and contributing to the learning of others."*
- ***Communication:*** *"Mastery of three fluencies: digital, writing, and speaking tailored for a range of audiences."*
- ***Creativity:*** *"Having an 'entrepreneurial eye' for economic and social opportunities, asking the right questions to generate novel ideas, and demonstrating leadership to pursue those ideas into practice."*
- ***Critical Thinking:*** *"Critically evaluating information and arguments, seeing patterns and connections, constructing meaningful knowledge and applying it in the real world." (pp. 6–7)*

Each of these competencies can be intentionally developed using various AI tools and applications. AI-powered tutoring systems with personalized feedback can strengthen character, helping students build perseverance and resilience as they address constructive criticism. Using AI tools, teachers can guide students to analyze current problems, explore how people with different backgrounds experience them, and develop solutions together, ultimately strengthening their citizenship skills in the process. AI tools that simulate complex team projects, monitor contributions, and analyze team dynamics can enhance collaboration and guide students in effective teamwork.

AI analysis enhances communication skills by refining tone, clarity, and impact across written, spoken, and digital messages for diverse audiences. Creativity is promoted through AI tools that support brainstorming, quick prototyping, and testing of innovative ideas in lifelike simulations. Critical thinking improves with AI research tools that assist students in evaluating sources, recognizing bias, and synthesizing data into solid conclusions. This transforms AI-powered learning environments into incubators for the Six C's, converting abstract goals into measurable, skill-based practices. By integrating human-centered values with future-ready skills, AI equips students to adapt to and influence a rapidly changing world.

Recognizing the importance of providing learners with opportunities to develop real-world skills is essential, especially as emerging technologies reshape the professional landscape. Careers that were non-existent or barely existed twenty-five years ago, such as AI engineer, social media strategist, or cybersecurity analyst, now dominate job boards. These roles require adaptability and proficiency in digital tools, many of which incorporate AI. This evolution underlines the need for education systems to respond not just with updated content, but with updated methods.

What do today's emerging professions have in common? In nearly every case, success requires a strong command of the "Six C's" of modern learning: creativity, communication, collaboration, critical thinking, character, and citizenship. Take, for example, a social media influencer. To be effective, they must think creatively and develop engaging content that captures attention in a crowded digital space. They need to communicate clearly to build trust and resonate with their audience. They often collaborate with brands, marketing teams, and fellow creators to produce and promote campaigns. Their work demands critical thinking to analyze engagement metrics, interpret trends, and adjust strategies. Finally, those who act with character and digital citizenship—promoting honesty, transparency, and social responsibility—tend to foster stronger, more enduring reputations.

Two decades ago, educators could not have predicted that their students would one day thrive in careers like these. And today, the full range of opportunities that await learners remains largely unforeseen. However, by equipping students with the "Six C's," educators prepare them not just for specific jobs, but for a world in constant motion—one that rewards adaptability, ethical decision-making, and the ability to create meaningful value in diverse and evolving contexts (Alaniz, 2021; Alaniz, 2024; Alaniz and Cerling, 2023).

The remaining sections of this chapter explore the formula for authentic learning, first introduced in *Collegial Coaching: Mentoring for Knowledge and Skills That Transfer to Real-world Applications* (Alaniz, 2021): authentic issues + authentic audiences + authentic assessment = authentic learning experiences.

Tackling Authentic Issues

In their daily lives, adults continually make decisions and solve problems, drawing on these real-world experiences to navigate everyday challenges and stay flexible in the face of change. However, many students enter adulthood without strong critical thinking or practical problem-solving skills, perhaps in part due to limited opportunities to develop these abilities in meaningful, authentic academic settings. Considering the significant amount of time students spend in school during their formative years, classrooms must provide rich opportunities for them to engage with authentic, relevant problems. Such practices develop students' cognitive skills while preparing them to manage the complexities inherent in adult life (Alaniz, 2021; Alaniz, 2024; Alaniz and Cerling, 2023).

Leveraging AI offers educators powerful capabilities to simulate authentic problems at scale, tailor challenges to student abilities, and provide real-time feedback. With AI's support, students can engage in realistic scenarios such as ethical decision-making in technology use, preparing them for a future where complex problem-solving is both expected and essential.

AI technologies are increasingly being used to help learners with writing, research, and solving problems, making learning more efficient and accessible. Yet, despite these advantages, they also introduce certain difficulties that must be carefully managed. When integrating When incorporating AI into learning environments, educators should create spaces that promote critical thinking, encouraging a balance between careful reflection and open exploration, while guiding students to consider:

- What information might be overlooked?
- How dependable is this result?
- What responsibilities come with using AI ethically? (University of Rhode Island, 2024)

Critical thinking has long served as a foundational element of education and intellectual growth. In an era shaped by AI, learners must move beyond simply relying on these tools; they need to grasp how to produce insights by validating information and recognizing both the potential and the constraints of digital tools and resources (University of Rhode Island, 2024).

When students apply critical thinking alongside AI integration, they become more effectively equipped to:

- *Think creatively and independently: Critical thinking encourages students to consider multiple perspectives and solutions, rather than simply relying on AI-generated answers. This independence nurtures innovation and personal insight.*
- *Distinguish fact from fabrication: While AI can generate vast amounts of text, not everything it produces is accurate. Encouraging students to fact-check and cross-reference helps cultivate a healthy skepticism.*
- *Challenge assumptions: AI often reflects only its training data. By guiding students to analyze the sources (including questioning potential biases) and recognize how assumptions shape information, it can help foster critical thinking. (para. 3)*

Important aspects to investigate regarding AI's limitations include:

- *Accuracy and Misinformation: AI produces results based on patterns in data rather than true understanding. Students may mistake plausible-sounding yet incorrect information for fact, undermining their knowledge and learning integrity.*
- *Data-Driven Biases: AI systems inherit biases from the data used to train them, potentially perpetuating skewed perspectives. Encouraging students to question these biases nurtures an awareness of how*

assumptions shape content, fostering a more discerning, balanced view of information.

- *Risks to Independent Thought: Over-relying on AI can hinder a student's own critical thinking skills. While AI might offer shortcuts, true learning often comes from grappling with complexity, not from accepting easy answers. (para. 4)*

Even amid the rise of AI, educators have significant opportunities to foster a spirit of inquiry among their students. The University of Rhode Island (2024) offers the following strategies to empower students to thoughtfully and critically engage with AI tools:

1. *Encourage source verification: Just as we ask students to cite sources in their own work, we can guide them to question AI sources and verify AI-generated content. This practice reinforces the importance of credible information and builds a habit of checking facts.*
2. *Examine AI's limitations together: Bring AI-generated outputs into class discussions, exploring where they succeed and where they fall short. This exercise helps students recognize that AI's "knowledge" is limited, often lacking the context, depth, and human judgment necessary for complex analysis.*
3. *Practice "spot the error" activities: Regularly review AI outputs in class to identify inaccuracies, ethical concerns, or biases. This approach not only develops a critical eye but reinforces the idea that AI should be questioned and evaluated, and not just passively accepted.*
4. *Engage in ethical dialogues: The ethics of AI use extend beyond academic integrity; it also includes privacy issues and potential societal impacts. Encouraging students to reflect on these implications fosters a responsible mindset, helping them consider the broader impact of their technology use. (para. 6)*

Encouraging students to build reflective habits and healthy skepticism toward AI enhances their ability to think independently. When AI complements, rather than replaces, human reasoning, it can boost critical thinking skills. This approach fosters a classroom setting in which technology is viewed as a valuable tool, not an unquestioned authority. In today's AI-rich world, nurturing critical thinking and intellectual independence is vital. Approaching AI with curiosity and caution enables students to use it responsibly and thoughtfully. Educators can help learners question information, analyze AI outputs, and practice analytical thinking, allowing their capacity for insight and inquiry to grow alongside technological progress (University of Rhode Island, 2024).

Engaging with Authentic Audiences

Just as students deepen their understanding when engaging with real-world issues, their learning becomes even more impactful when it is shared with authentic audiences, especially when AI tools support and amplify those experiences. Presenting work beyond the classroom not only elevates relevance but, when powered by AI, also opens powerful opportunities for personalization, feedback, and broader reach. AI-infused platforms enable students to interact with virtual or global audiences, simulate real-world presentation settings, and refine their work using predictive and generative technologies.

Authentic learning experiences empower students to showcase knowledge and skills in purposeful ways. With AI, students can practice interviewing virtual experts, create and test simple digital prototypes, and use language tools to improve their writing and communication. The prospect of sharing learning products with real-world viewers—whether peers, community members, industry professionals, or global online audiences—often inspires deeper engagement and higher-quality work. In today's increasingly connected world, digital tools expand the avenues for learners to present their thinking far beyond school walls.

In alignment with the Understanding by Design model, the process of identifying an appropriate audience begins with clarifying the intended learning outcomes. After first determining what students should know and be able to do, educators should then select a project format that aligns with those goals, potentially recruiting students to help with the selection process. For instance, students might collaborate to address a local community issue using principles learned in social studies or analyze a contemporary topic explored in history class. By defining the learning outcomes early, educators can more easily identify audiences for whom the final product will be relevant, meaningful, and impactful (Alaniz, 2021; Alaniz, 2024; Alaniz and Cerling, 2023).

AI can enhance this alignment process by analyzing student strengths, identifying relevant content gaps, and even recommending project formats or presentation styles based on learning analytics. Additionally, generative AI tools can help students develop scripts, visuals, and multimedia presentations that meet the needs and preferences of diverse audiences.

The significance of allowing learners to present to various audiences is explored in *Collegial Coaching: Mentoring for Knowledge and Skills That Transfer to Real-World Applications* (Alaniz, 2021):

> *Authentic audiences should vary from project to project, providing students with opportunities to apply developing skills in the presence of different groups of people. Teachers may begin by seeking familiar audience members, such as family, friends, or others who already have an interest in students' lives. Learners might also present their creations to others within the school setting, such as students in other classes or grade levels as well as administrators or instructional support specialists. It may also be helpful to seek the support of experts in the field. For example, students working on an impressionist painting project in art class might host a gallery walk and invite a local artist to tour the exhibit. (p. 97)*

AI tools can further broaden access to these diverse audiences. Students can create digital gallery walks, share their work in moderated online spaces where a teacher reviews posts and guides discussion, or practice pitching their projects to AI-simulated stakeholders using real-world information. Language translation and accessibility tools also enable students to reach global audiences, thereby transcending physical and linguistic barriers.

Mathtrain.TV (http://mathtrain.tv/) exemplifies how engaging with real audiences motivates students to produce meaningful work. At Lincoln Middle School in Santa Monica, California, students collaborate to create math screencasts that are featured on the site, reaching viewers worldwide. While making these popular videos, students use critical thinking to clearly explain their problem-solving methods.

Mathtrain.TV has attracted over sixty thousand viewers globally. This clearly shows the impact of authentic audiences. It is easy to imagine the motivation and confidence students at Lincoln Middle School experience, knowing their

Figure 5.1 Mathtrain.TV QR Code.

math tutorials influence thousands they may never meet. Now, with the support of AI, such efforts can be expanded further. AI can help students storyboard their content, generate accessible captions, and even analyze viewer engagement to iterate on future projects. Students not only see the relevance of their work, but they also begin to understand how data, communication, and feedback loops intersect in real-world digital environments.

Designing Effective Authentic Assessments

While engaging with a real audience provides students with a sense of purpose, it is authentic assessment that gives their work structure and substance. These assessments encourage learners to showcase their understanding in diverse, meaningful formats, closely mirroring the demands of real-world performance.

In the words of Alaniz (2021),

> *[Authentic assessment] provides a revealing glimpse of what learners actually know and what they can actually do, rather than showcasing how skillfully students can take quizzes or exams. Authentic assessments provide opportunities for learners to create novel end products, rather than simply requiring that they consume information for the purpose of regurgitating it while taking a quiz or exam. (p. 98)*

Amoush and Farhat (2023) offer a number of examples of authentic assessment strategies that incorporate the principles shared throughout this chapter and may include varying degrees of AI integration, including the following:

- Student demonstrations: Students showcase their learning by conducting experiments, writing original narratives, building models or prototypes, or performing self-scripted plays. These activities require research, promote the application of diverse learning styles, and allow students to highlight their strengths and interests.

- Student collaboration: Students work together on projects that require teamwork, taking on specific roles and responsibilities. Teams plan and hold regular meetings, document their progress for instructor feedback, and refine their work before presenting. Each member reports on their contributions and how they supported the overall outcome, sharing results with the class, the instructor, or an authentic audience such as a community group or academic panel.
- Empirical research: Students collect and analyze data related to a learning objective using methods such as interviews, observations, or focus groups. They present evidence, including photographs, videos, and statistics, to an authentic audience, explaining their process and responding to questions.
- Presentations: Students prepare and deliver oral presentations such as debates, seminars, or panel discussions. These activities require evidence-based analysis, anticipation of counterarguments, and the ability to respond thoughtfully, thereby strengthening higher-order thinking skills.
- Media production: Students create documentaries, podcasts, or videos to communicate their understanding of course content in engaging and accessible ways.
- Teaching peers: Students take on the role of instructor, teaching a concept or skill from the course to peers or other groups. This requires a deep understanding of the material as well as the ability to simplify and clearly explain complex ideas.
- Role-playing: Students demonstrate their learning through creative formats such as poems, sketches, stories, songs, paintings, mind maps, or cartoons, offering alternatives to traditional essays or oral reports.
- Reenactments: Students recreate historical events or other significant moments, such as political agreements, to demonstrate understanding of context, sequence, and significance.
- Exhibitions and fairs: Students present their learning products, such as posters, paintings, photographs, collages, models, prototypes, or portfolios, in a public showcase. They explain their process and respond to audience questions.

With the support of AI tools, students can enhance the quality and creativity of their authentic assessments. For example, when creating a multimedia presentation, learners might use AI to produce high-quality visuals, outline their content, or rehearse their delivery with speech analysis features. In designing a public awareness campaign, they could leverage AI-generated taglines or storyboard templates to kickstart their ideas. During interviews or surveys, students might utilize AI to summarize results, discover patterns, or visualize data. These tools do not replace student thinking; instead, they amplify it by offering scaffolds that save time, inspire new ideas, and enable a deeper focus on content and meaning.

Authentic assessment serves as an effective means of navigating the various implications of the increased AI use in educational contexts. These assessments more accurately gauge student learning and equip learners for real-world challenges by emphasizing practical application, critical thinking, creativity, communication, collaboration, citizenship, and character development. Although they require more effort to create and assess, their benefits for student engagement, motivation, and understanding make them essential to current educational practices. Educators can leverage AI's potential by adopting authentic assessments while upholding academic integrity and promoting significant learning experiences (Snipes, 2024).

Essential Ideas to Remember

Authentic learning empowers students by linking educational activities to real-world contexts, thereby boosting their engagement in academic endeavors. AI offers new possibilities for enhancing how students engage with learning resources, creating opportunities to weave digital literacy, critical thinking, and problem-solving into their studies. By deliberately integrating AI into lesson planning, educators can foster students' skills in analyzing and judging AI-produced content rather than merely accepting it without question. This transition not only sharpens their critical thinking abilities but also equips them for a rapidly changing job market that demands digital proficiency.

A key framework for meaningful learning is built upon the following formula: authentic issues + authentic audiences + authentic assessment = authentic learning experiences (Alaniz, 2021). When students engage with real-world problems, present their work to genuine audiences, and participate in assessments that reflect real-life applications, they move from passive recipients of knowledge to active contributors. Educators must begin with a clear purpose, ensuring students see the relevance of each concept they learn. This intrinsic motivation fosters deeper engagement and resilience.

AI tools offer both opportunities and challenges in education. While they provide students with unprecedented access to information and support in problem-solving, they also introduce concerns related to accuracy, bias, and over-reliance. To develop independent thinkers, educators must guide students in questioning AI-generated content, verifying sources, and recognizing the limitations of these technologies. Encouraging inquiry-based learning ensures that students do not view AI as an infallible authority but as a tool to enhance their critical reasoning.

Authentic learning also involves engaging with real audiences, which increases students' motivation and the quality of their work. Learners often take greater ownership of their work as they understand that audiences beyond only their teacher will view their projects. Students gain valuable communication skills and a stronger sense of purpose when presenting to classmates, school administrators, community members, or even global audiences through digital platforms. Digital tools have expanded these opportunities, allowing students to share their learning in meaningful ways.

Assessment plays a crucial role in authentic learning, shifting the focus from rote memorization to real-world application. Authentic assessments require students to demonstrate their understanding through hands-on projects, presentations, role-playing, research, and creative expressions. When integrated effectively with AI, these assessments can reinforce skills such as collaboration, problem-solving, and adaptability. While designing and evaluating such assessments may demand greater effort from educators, he long-term advantages include enhanced engagement, stronger learning results, and heightened readiness for the challenges of the future.

Ultimately, AI is reshaping education, and it is imperative that educators strike a balance between leveraging its benefits and fostering independent thought. By embracing authentic learning experiences, incorporating real-world problem-solving, engaging diverse audiences, and designing meaningful assessments, teachers can prepare students to navigate an AI-influenced world with confidence, curiosity, and integrity.

References

Alaniz, K. (2021). *Collegial Coaching: Mentoring for Knowledge and Skills That Transfer to Real-World Applications*. Bloomsbury.

Alaniz, K. (2024). *A Learning Community Built on Strengths: Inspiring Educators to Positively Impact Student Lives*. Bloomsbury.

Alaniz, K. and K. Cerling (2023). *Authentic Assessment in Action: An Everyday Guide for Bringing Learning to Life Through Meaningful Assessment*. Bloomsbury.

Amoush, S.A. and A. Farhat (2023, December 13). "The Power of Authentic Assessment in the Age of AI." *Faculty Focus*. https://www.facultyfocus.com/articles/educational-assessment/the-power-of-authentic-assessment-in-the-age-of-ai/.

Dolbin, R.J., L. Ying, R. Slabbinck, and R.L. Stewart (2024, November). *AI-Powered Education: Authentic Assessments and Learning*. Academic Senate for California Community Colleges. https://www.asccc.org/content/ai-powered-education-authentic-assessments-and-learning.

Fullan, M. and G. Scott (2014). *New Pedagogies for Deep Learning Whitepaper: Education PLUS*. Collaborative Impact SPC.

Snipes, S. (2024, July 29). *Authentic Assessment: A Powerful Tool to Manage AI Use in Education*. LinkedIn. https://www.linkedin.com/pulse/authentic-assessment-powerful-tool-manage-ai-use-shane-snipes-ph-d–368ce/.

University of Rhode Island (2024, November 25). "Empowering Students: Critical Thinking Can Balance Curiosity and Caution with AI." University of Rhode Island. https://its.uri.edu/2024/11/25/empowering-students-critical-thinking-can-balance-curiosity-and-caution-with-ai/.

6 Ethical Implications of AI in Education

Equipping Responsible and Informed Digital Citizens

"Technology doesn't just change what we do. It changes who we are."
SHERRY TURKLE

At a time when artificial intelligence is redefining how humans live, learn, and connect, the classroom is becoming an essential space for guiding students in ethical decision-making. As educators adopt advanced tools to enhance teaching, they also face challenging questions about student safety, data privacy, and the impact of human insight on the learning process. This chapter examines how AI in education drives innovation while also serving as a test of ethical responsibility, highlighting the measures that must be taken to protect and empower students in a world where digital and human elements are increasingly entwined.

AI in education—particularly generative AI (GenAI)—presents transformative potential but also raises significant ethical concerns, including overreliance on AI tools, data privacy, and equitable access (Moquin, 2024). Effectively responding to these concerns calls for a deliberate approach to ensure that AI enhances learning while maintaining fairness and trust. As academic institutions increasingly adopt AI solutions, the ethical implications must be carefully considered.

As explored in the book *Collegial Coaching: Mentoring for Knowledge and Skills That Transfer to Real-world Applications* (Alaniz, 2021),

In educational environments, the promise of digital integration is vast. It holds the potential to advance learning opportunities for students around the world… It provides teachers with groundbreaking tools for reimagining the transfer of key concepts, thereby inspiring students to become co-creators of their own learning endeavors. The issue resides in the fact that technology incorporation fluctuates depending on the content area at hand and the developmental levels involved in the learning. (p. 42)

AI presents transformative opportunities for education, but its impact depends on intentional, purposeful implementation aligned with clear learning goals. Simply introducing AI tools into classrooms is not enough; educators, students, and school communities must understand why and how these technologies enhance learning. When thoughtfully applied, AI can personalize instruction, deepen student engagement, and support data-informed decision-making.

Without a clear pedagogical rationale, however, AI risks becoming a distraction rather than a driver of innovation. Preparing students for the future requires immersing them in forward-thinking, ethical, and impactful learning experiences today. This means school districts, educators, and families must critically evaluate the use of emerging technologies, not based on trends, but on their true potential to benefit students and transform learning in meaningful ways.

In the words of Moquin (2024),

Ethical AI in education means designing, using, and managing AI tools in a way that puts people first—focusing on fairness, transparency, and the well-being of students and educators. It's about ensuring that these powerful technologies help, rather than harm, the learning experience. For example, when an AI system evaluates a student's performance or helps tailor their learning, ethical AI ensures those decisions are free from bias and based on accurate, fair data. It also means respecting students' and teachers' privacy—guarding personal information and being clear about its use. But ethics in AI aren't just about the tech itself. They're about people and policies. Schools, educators, and even governments play a role in setting rules and expectations to ensure AI supports equity, inclusion, and trust in education. By thinking beyond technology, we can ensure AI is a tool for progress, not a source of unintended harm. (paras. 4–6)

Fundamental Ethical Considerations Related to AI in Academia

AI in education brings ethical challenges that must be addressed with care. Chief concerns surrounding the use of AI in education involve the possible spread of flawed or inaccurate information, risks to student data privacy, insufficient transparency, and the danger of becoming overly dependent on automated technologies (Moquin, 2024). These issues often arise when AI systems are trained on incomplete or biased data or are poorly designed.

AI systems often accumulate large datasets on students, which may include identifying details, educational histories, and behavioral trends. This data can help personalize learning or streamline operations, but it also carries significant privacy risks. Unprotected or misused data may lead to breaches or commercial exploitation. To prevent this, institutions must practice transparency, seek informed consent, and communicate clearly with students and families about what data is collected, how it is used, and how it is protected (Moquin, 2024).

Moquin (2024) also stresses the importance of professional development. Educators need robust training to understand how AI works, identify potential flaws, and use these tools responsibly. Such training empowers them to align AI use with pedagogical goals while promoting fairness and critical reflection in the classroom. Institutional safeguards are equally essential. Schools should adopt clear data privacy policies, enforce strong cybersecurity measures, and regularly review AI practices for ethical compliance. Obtaining consent from students or guardians and maintaining transparency throughout helps build a culture of trust (Moquin, 2024).

Ultimately, ethical integration of AI begins with a clear purpose. Starting with the WHY and using frameworks such as the upcoming TPACK framework to guide implementation, educators can ensure that digital innovation enhances rather than hampers learning.

Grounding AI in Pedagogy by Applying the TPACK Framework

To effectively incorporate AI in the classroom, educators need to base their use of digital tools on solid pedagogical principles, such as the TPACK framework (Herring, Koehler, and Mishra, 2016). This model highlights that purposeful technology use starts with clear instructional goals. Without clear guidance, even the most sophisticated tools can be misused, ultimately hindering student learning.

TPACK links three key areas: content knowledge (CK), pedagogical knowledge (PK), and technological knowledge (TK). Instead of viewing them separately, TPACK emphasizes their overlaps, where educators can make the most informed instructional choices. These overlaps include pedagogical content knowledge (PCK), technological content knowledge (TCK), technological pedagogical knowledge (TPK), and ultimately, technological pedagogical content knowledge (TPACK).

As Alaniz (2021) observes, successful technology use hinges on effective pedagogy and a deep understanding of learner needs. Each classroom context is unique, shaped by individual students, diverse demographics, shifting environments, and subject-specific goals. Therefore, no single configuration of content, pedagogy, and technology will be universally effective.

The following descriptions, adapted from Koehler (2012), define the components of the TPACK framework:

- **Content Knowledge (CK):** Educators' strong command of their subject, including facts, concepts, theories, and structures within a discipline.
- **Pedagogical Knowledge (PK):** Broad expertise in teaching strategies, classroom management, lesson planning, and assessment that supports effective learning.
- **Technology Knowledge (TK):** The capacity to choose, use, and evaluate appropriate technological tools to support instructional goals.
- **Pedagogical Content Knowledge (PCK):** The ability to teach specific content effectively, translating subject matter into meaningful learning experiences.

- **Technological Content Knowledge (TCK):** Understanding how technology can support or reshape the way content is presented and explored.
- **Technological Pedagogical Knowledge (TPK):** Insight into how particular technologies interact with teaching methods to influence student engagement and outcomes.
- **Technological Pedagogical Content Knowledge (TPACK):** The integration of all three domains—content, pedagogy, and technology—to deliver instruction that is both meaningful and adaptive.

When educators apply the TPACK model, they go beyond basic technology use to purposeful, student-focused integration. For example, a teacher might use video materials to support visual and auditory learners or create interactive lessons with multimodal tools to address diverse learning needs. As Alaniz (2021) notes, technology should support learning goals, not replace or distract from them.

Ultimately, the TPACK framework supports educators in venturing beyond simply using digital tools for their novelty, directing them to make instructional decisions that combine content, pedagogy, and technology. Purposeful use of AI, aligned with specific learning objectives, promotes meaningful and contextually relevant student engagement.

Designing Assessment with Purpose in the Age of AI

As AI and other digital tools become more integrated into educational settings, the importance of careful assessment increases. Educators need to evaluate not just student learning but also how AI-supported instruction and creation influence outcomes. Therefore, assessments should be deliberately aligned with learning objectives and clearly communicate expectations and results.

Before initiating the assessment process, educators should identify the purpose of the digital resource. For teacher-created tools, effectiveness can be evaluated by how well the resource supports instructional objectives and leads to measurable learning gains. Informal strategies, such as KWL charts, can capture shifts in student understanding, while pre- and post-assessments provide more formal indicators of content mastery.

When students create AI-supported digital media, such as written content, presentations, or interactive projects, both the process and the final product should be evaluated. This includes evaluating how responsibly and purposefully students used AI tools, as well as how effectively their work demonstrates content understanding and skill development.

As explained by Wilson, Alaniz, and Sikora (2016),

> *The process of assessing student-created digital media pieces entails a somewhat different perspective and premise. Teachers must determine not only whether the process of multimedia creation supports students in learning, but they must also ascertain how effectively the end product demonstrates acquired knowledge and skills. Skillfully designed criteria-based rubrics enable students to comprehend specifically how their work will be evaluated, even before they begin the project. This way, students—and not just their teachers—receive the opportunity to "begin with the end in mind," focusing more specifically and purposefully on meeting predetermined criteria for excellence, rather than blindly and haphazardly piecing together their projects. (p. 119)*

This approach is especially valuable in AI-enhanced learning. When educators provide clear rubrics in advance, students are better equipped to use AI as a tool to support, rather than replace, their thinking. Rubrics should address both the quality of content and the student's ability to use AI ethically and effectively. This might include criteria for appropriate prompting, attribution of AI-generated content, and demonstration of original thought and reflection.

By integrating purposeful assessment with clear guidelines for AI use, educators can foster deeper learning, digital literacy, and responsible innovation. For more information on rubric development and assessment strategies, Chapter 4 provides additional tools to ensure that evaluations remain fair, focused, and student-centered in digitally dynamic classrooms.

Evaluating AI-Enhanced Digital Projects by Balancing Substance, Structure, and Style

As students use AI tools to create digital learning artifacts, it becomes more vital for educators and learners to evaluate not only the content but also the structure and visual quality of those projects. AI can help generate ideas, suggest formats, or produce drafts, but students must ultimately use critical thinking to improve, select, and customize their final work. The success of these projects depends on how effectively students combine content with digital design elements, including subtexts, images, music, and videos.

In the words of Wilson, Alaniz, and Sikora (2016),

> *Unquestionably, issues arise when form contradicts content, potentially leading to audience confusion or distraction from the main message. For instance, if teachers expect students to create a video summarizing the content of a book but give no criteria for evaluating the grammatical and mechanical aspects of the text included within the video, learners may more likely ignore these important aspects of multimedia creation. Ultimately, poorly written text might distract from an otherwise well-designed video, thus causing viewers to overlook key content. (pp. 120–1)*

AI may assist in generating text or visuals, but it does not eliminate the responsibility students have in ensuring that the final product communicates clearly and aligns with academic standards. Educators must guide students to assess both the substance and style of their work, even when AI tools are part of the creative process. Key factors for evaluating content include:

- *Content accuracy: Are the facts presented verifiable? Were they taken from valid and reliable sources?*
- *Content clarity: Does the final product convey a central theme or themes? Do the individual pieces serve to enhance one cohesive whole?*
- *Content creativity: Did the designer add certain unique elements to demonstrate his or her ability to innovate? What aspects of this project differentiate it from the others submitted?*
- *Content purposes: Do content and form align, or does form distract from the key messages of the content?*

- *Copyright considerations: Did the student adequately and accurately cite resources used throughout the presentation, including text, image, music, and video clips? Is it apparent that the student sought to abide by fair use considerations, being careful to avoid too extensively using any one audio or video segment? (Wilson, Alaniz, and Sikora, 2016, p. 121)*

Although AI can assist in quickly assembling content or generating visuals, the final responsibility for coherence and originality rests with the student. A visually polished product that lacks accuracy or context may be just as problematic as a strong concept poorly executed. Presentation quality also plays a critical role in how audiences receive and interpret digital messages. Students must learn to evaluate the visual and structural elements that impact the effectiveness of their work. AI tools may suggest designs or transitions, but students should be taught to review and refine them intentionally. When considering aesthetic quality, learners should focus on the following indicators:

- *Font consistency: Do the style and size of the font increase readability and align with the theme of the project, or do they detract from the central message?*
- *Template consistency: How well do the chosen templates align with the key ideas conveyed through the multimedia piece? Do they support a central theme or seem disjointed?*
- *Animation or transitional consistency: Do animations and transitions add interest to the project and enhance audience engagement, or might they potentially befuddle and/or distract viewers?*
- *Color and style consistency: How effectively do other visual elements, such as color palettes and the style of the finished product, support the chief ideas expressed? Do they serve to draw attention to significant themes, or do they seem out of place?*
- *Image choices: Does the presentation contain high-quality images that support the audience in visualizing a central message, or do the images seem fuzzy and/or out of place in consideration of the prevailing theme? (Wilson, Alaniz, and Sikora, 2016, pp. 121–2)*

When students use AI to generate images or design suggestions, they must be guided to critically evaluate what the tool offers. A strong final product reflects thoughtful curation and intentional decisions, not just automation. In today's world, where video creation is increasingly common in both education and professional industries, students should develop experience in both live and recorded presentation formats. AI may assist with scripting or editing, but students still need a deep understanding of the components that make a video effective and engaging. Evaluating video-based presentations involves additional dimensions, including:

- *Technical quality: Does the video contain clear, applicable images, organized in a logical format? Are the exposure levels suitable, and was the camera held steady throughout shooting?*
- *Audio quality: Are the sound levels appropriate throughout the video? Does the narration and music blend well, or is the volume of one element disproportionate?*
- *Engaging quality: Do the text, image, narration, music, and video elements work cohesively to capture audience interest? Does the video contain developmental, dynamic aspects that maintain viewers' curiosity and attentiveness?*
- *Cinematic quality: Does the video contain a transportive quality, serving as a vehicle to transfer viewers' minds to another place and time? Is there an element of journalistic style, conveying accuracy, brevity, and candor? How do motion, images, lighting, and color intermingle to add visual appeal to the piece? In what ways do sound and musical elements enhance the emotions inspired by the video? How is editing utilized to inspire intellectual curiosity and a sense of wonder? (Wilson, Alaniz, and Sikora, 2016, p. 123)*

Ultimately, AI should support students in enhancing their creativity, not replace the need for thoughtful design, ethical choices, and intentional messaging. When assessment emphasizes both what is communicated and how it is presented, students are better prepared to be discerning creators in a digital world shaped by both human insight and intelligent tools.

Empowering Learners Through Innovation and AI-Aware Pedagogy

Identifying appropriate digital tools and learning resources was once both time-consuming and labor-intensive. However, this is no longer true in an environment shaped by bring-your-own-device (BYOD) programs, widespread Wi-Fi access, and the rapid growth of AI platforms. Today, educators and learners have instant access to a broad range of powerful technologies, including AI tools that can generate text, images, code, and data-driven insights. Still, despite this availability, challenges remain in gaining the critical competencies to use these tools responsibly, ethically, and effectively in both educational settings and daily life.

As with many aspects of educational change, straightforward solutions are often elusive. Introducing AI into schools adds complexity that calls for careful thought and ethical considerations. Among these concerns, ensuring students are safe—both physically and digitally—becomes a top priority for educators committed to cultivating the growth of future generations in a world increasingly influenced by AI.

As noted by Wilson, Alaniz, and Sikora (2016),

> *Just as administrators, faculty, and staff members are responsible for the physical safety of the students under their care at school each day, they are also liable for the online safety of these students. By the same token, as teachers instinctively guide their students in becoming responsible citizens of the communities in which they live, they must also learn to lead today's younger generations in developing the mindsets and habits of responsible digital and global citizens… While many forward-thinking teachers delight in the prospect of introducing innovative, engaging digital tools to their students, fewer numbers consider the imperative of doing so in correlation with instruction in digital citizenship. Yet, these two endeavors must go hand in hand. (p. 34)*

This urgency is heightened by the extensive adoption of AI. These tools can revolutionize learning by supporting brainstorming, tutoring, text summarization, and real-world simulations. Nonetheless, they prompt serious considerations related to data privacy, misinformation, intellectual property, and dependency. As students become more dependent on AI-powered platforms, educators must proactively encourage responsible AI use, helping students critically evaluate how these tools influence their thinking, outputs, and digital identities.

Effective collaboration among administrators, digital learning specialists, IT leaders, and curriculum coordinators is crucial. These stakeholders can support educators and parents in becoming better informed and more proactive about student privacy, tudent privacy and the ethical use of AI, and the ethical use of AI. Such teamwork also encourages students to take responsibility for their online actions, promoting resilience, agency, and awareness in the digital world.

Fortunately, there is an increasing availability of comprehensive resources dedicated to digital safety education and AI literacy. For instance, Common Sense Media (https://www.commonsensemedia.org/) consistently provides relevant materials covering privacy, digital well-being, and the rights and responsibilities of students as both content creators and consumers in a world enhanced by AI.

Safeguarding Student Privacy in a Generative AI World

The Children's Online Privacy Protection Act (COPPA), administered by the Federal Trade Commission, is designed to safeguard the digital privacy and safety of young learners. COPPA specifically limits the collection of personal information from children under 13 years old, placing legal obligations on website and service operators. Although rooted in US law, its reach is global, affecting the practices of individuals, educational institutions, and businesses worldwide.

Figure 6.1 Common Sense Media QR Code.

COPPA outlines strict responsibilities for online platforms, including the need to present clear privacy policies and secure verifiable parental consent prior to collecting any data. These protections are designed to shield children from unwanted data exposure and targeted marketing. In an era where AI tools are being rapidly introduced into classrooms, these guidelines become even more essential. AI systems often involve large-scale data processing, and their integration in schools raises new questions about student data security, consent, algorithmic transparency, and usage boundaries.

Figure 6.2 COPPA Overview. Video presentation explaining the Children's Online Privacy Protection Act QR Code.

> *As guardians of the well-being of future generations, school stakeholders must consider strategies for involving students, parents, and community members in developing a culture of online safety and digital citizenship, in K–12 settings and beyond.... Some schools and districts designate campus personnel, such as digital learning specialists or technology directors, as those responsible for reviewing the Terms of Service/Terms of Use and privacy policies of the websites teachers desire to use within their classrooms. (Wilson, Alaniz, and Sikora, 2016, pp. 37–8)*

The growing popularity of AI-powered learning tools has intensified the need for rigorous review processes. Educators and educational leaders now play a dual role: selecting effective tools for instruction and shaping policies and practices to ensure their responsible use in compliance with COPPA.

> *Faculty members may be invited to share suggested sites with these designated community members, allowing another set of eyes to review terms and privacy policies before new sites are introduced to the students.... These suggestions, of course, represent only a start to safeguarding students' online privacy and protection. Educational organizations, districts, and schools still need to deliver richer, more applicable teacher and parent education regarding the specifics of student data and privacy. (Alaniz, Wilson, and Sikora, 2016, pp. 38–9)*

As more educators utilize AI to enhance teaching through personalized learning, content support, and the illustration of complex reasoning, student privacy, ethics, and digital boundaries must be prioritized. Because AI tools often record interactions or require access to personal data, conflicts can arise with COPPA regulations unless appropriate safeguards and parental consent are in place.

To stay compliant, educators must ensure that any digital tools used in the classroom adhere to COPPA requirements, have clear and transparent privacy policies, and obtain parental consent when necessary, before collecting student data. Students, in turn, need guidance to understand how these tools work and how to use them responsibly. Although AI offers powerful capabilities, it also poses risks such as overdependence, misinformation, and bias stemming from training data. Educators play an important part in supporting students as they think critically and make sense of these complex issues.

Promoting digital citizenship in the age of AI is now a core responsibility, not an optional add-on. Schools need to cultivate a culture of learning that incorporates the ethical use of AI, privacy awareness, and data literacy into their daily instructional practice. However, this duty should not rest only on classroom teachers. Effective collaboration among administrators, IT leaders, digital learning experts, and families is crucial for creating safe, future-ready learning environments. Educational communities can collaborate to verify that AI tools are implemented in a manner that prioritizes student safety, maintains instructional quality, and fosters digital empowerment. As always, teamwork makes the dream work.

Educators, institutions, and families share the duty of ensuring AI serves to enhance, rather than replace, student thinking. With careful integration, a clear purpose, collaborative safeguards, and frameworks such as TPACK, AI can facilitate transformative learning experiences. Focusing on privacy, fairness, and student agency allows schools to equip learners not simply to utilize AI effectively, but to understand and actively participate in shaping the future it is helping to construct.

Essential Ideas to Remember

The integration of AI in education offers numerous possibilities while also introducing notable challenges. While it can enhance learning experiences through personalized instruction and automation, it also raises ethical concerns, including privacy, accuracy, and overreliance. Responsible AI use requires careful ethical consideration. Establishing clear guidelines and safeguards can help prevent misuse while fostering trust among students and educators.

Adaptability is essential; as technology advances, students and educators must cultivate expanding digital literacy. Successful AI integration depends on collaboration among policymakers, educators, students, and technology developers. Ultimately, the goal of AI in education should be to empower students rather than replace human ingenuity and critical thinking.

References

Alaniz, K. (2021). *Collegial Coaching: Mentoring for Knowledge and Skills That Transfer to Real-World Applications*. Bloomsbury.

Herring, M.C., M.J. Koehler, and P. Mishra (2016). *Handbook of Technological Pedagogical Content Knowledge (TPACK) for Educators* (2nd ed.). Routledge.

Koehler, M.J. (2012, September 24). *TPACK Explained*. Retrieved from https://matt-koehler.com/tpack2/tpack-explained/.

Moquin, S. (2024, November 26). "Ethical Considerations for AI Use in Education." *Enrollify*. https://www.enrollify.org/blog/ethical-considerations-for-ai-use-in-education.

Wilson, D., K. Alaniz, and J. Sikora (2016). *Digital Media in Today's Classrooms: The Potential for Meaningful Teaching, Learning, and Assessment*. Bloomsbury.

7 Thriving with AI

Transforming Classrooms and Cultivating Purpose Through Authentic Learning

"Technology will never replace great teachers,
but in the hands of great teachers, it's transformational."
GEORGE COUROS

Faculty development programs and curriculum designers have long championed applicable, authentic learning experiences, but the need for such approaches has never been greater. With students now having access to advanced AI tools capable of rapidly producing complete assignments, educators must respond swiftly and decisively to ensure submitted work reflects genuine student effort rather than solely AI output. This commitment is essential to preserving the integrity of assessments and ensuring they fulfill their primary purpose: supporting students in achieving the intended learning outcomes (Amoush and Farhat, 2023).

Authentic learning experiences are especially valuable in the age of AI, helping teachers and students meet this goal by mirroring real-world tasks learners will encounter beyond the classroom. Such activities engage students with authentic audiences and responsibilities that reflect their future professional and personal lives, requiring them to produce meaningful artifacts of learning rather than simply answering questions or responding to prompts (Amoush and Farhat, 2023).

Designing such tasks requires thoughtful integration of collaboration among peers, opportunities for self and peer assessment, and diverse methods for presenting their findings. Additionally, self-reflection is crucial for helping students thoughtfully consider their learning journey, assess their progress, and understand how their new knowledge fits into the broader context of their lives beyond educational settings (Amoush and Farhat, 2023).

When educators intentionally cultivate meaningful and AI-enhanced learning experiences for their students, they unlock the full potential of today's digital tools to transform the learning environment. By committing to applicable, purposeful integration of AI and other digital resources, educators can significantly influence classroom culture and inspire campus-wide innovation, leaving a lasting impact on the lives of today's learners.

The effective use of digital technologies, including AI, provides many benefits in education, like enabling personalized learning experiences. For example, by recognizing individual needs and skills, AI facilitates customized lesson plans, recommends suitable resources, and identifies areas where students need additional support (Moquin, 2024). AI-powered systems can tailor reading suggestions to suit each learner's skill level or adjust the speed of a math program based on individual progress. This personalized approach helps boost academic achievement and ensures that students feel valued and supported. By automating routine tasks, teachers can devote more time to instruction, guidance, and fostering meaningful connections with their students, ultimately enriching the learning experience (Moquin, 2024).

Authentic learning endeavors provide educators with a clear vision and practical pathway for designing relevant, personalized, and impactful learning experiences. By leveraging AI to adapt instruction, recommend resources, and assess progress in real time, educators can better guide students toward achieving their learning aspirations. As students engage in these tailored, meaningful experiences, their confidence and enthusiasm for learning grow, encouraging them to share their achievements and insights with peers. Over time, AI-supported environments promote reciprocal learning by using adaptive tools that pair students for collaboration, deliver real-time feedback, and guide them to alternate between learner and facilitator roles. These collaborative, tech-enhanced interactions hold the potential to deepen understanding and create valuable reciprocal learning opportunities for all learners.

Cultivating the Joy of Learning in the Age of AI

Many students view learning as an obligation rather than a source of genuine enjoyment. For those who feel disconnected from classroom experiences, school can seem like a chore rather than a meaningful opportunity. Considering the thousands of hours students spend in school throughout their academic lives, this disconnection is troubling. AI-powered tools can help address this by enabling more authentic, relevant learning experiences that reflect students' interests, strengths, and needs. When learning is personalized and aligned with real-world contexts through the use of AI, student motivation and engagement increase, transforming schools into places of discovery and joy.

As explained by Professor John Wang (2017) of the National Institute of Education,

> *When students look for "interesting" teachers and classrooms, they are in fact looking for an environment that caters to their core needs for autonomy, competence, and relatedness. They look for teachers who are able to meet their needs and interests and who can create interesting and challenging lessons that are relevant to their lives. A classroom where "joy of learning" exists is one in which students are given appropriate levels of challenges and one in which they are able to make decisions about their learning… When they experience "joy of learning", students benefit from a positive learning experience. From the teacher's perspective, it would always be more rewarding if students were motivated and eager to learn: When teachers see motivated students, they too, become more interested to teach. (p. 1)*

Genuine learning experiences, including those enhanced by AI, not only increase student enjoyment but also provide educators with a more profound sense of purpose and fulfillment. Rather than being limited by rigid curricula and standardized assessments, teachers can leverage AI to create dynamic, student-centered opportunities that support creativity, innovation, and critical thinking. When students are empowered to become active participants in their learning, using AI to explore, create, and reflect, they grow into confident, capable learners.

As described by Timperley and Schick (2025),

> *As part of an ontological approach to teaching and learning, we recognise the integrated nature of all that we do as course instructors and learners, from course design to classroom dynamics to assessment. Assessment, we argue, should be concerned with what makes us human, and uplift those dimensions of our beings that we seek to cultivate as humans, in particular our curiosity, joy, and relationships with others. Rather than focusing primarily on demonstrating the acquisition of knowledge or skills via summative or formative assessment processes, we advocate creating space for students 'to embody and affectively experience knowledge' (Gravett, Taylor, and Fairchild, 2024, 399) via innovative practices such as creative assessments. (pp. 595–6)*

A powerful example of nurturing the joy of learning through authentic strategies that incorporate digital tools and resources in EC-12 educational settings is digital storytelling. These multimedia narratives combine text, narration, images, music, and videos to convey meaning. Many free, online tools are available for creating digital stories, enabling learners of all ages to produce significant learning artifacts.

In addition to digital storytelling, educators can adopt various authentic learning strategies that utilize AI tools to enhance creativity, teamwork, and real-world relevance. For example, students can create podcasts by researching, scripting, and producing episodes related to their own lives or communities, often with the aid of AI for brainstorming or editing. AI-assisted role-playing simulations can immerse learners in historical, scientific, or civic scenarios where they must make decisions based on live feedback or changing data.

Collaborative design challenges encourage students to address real-world issues, such as sustainability, accessibility, or community needs, by working in teams to develop prototypes using AI-powered research or design tools. Other effective methods include building digital portfolios, conducting community research projects, or crafting interactive presentations with AI-enhanced visuals or data storytelling. These approaches not only deepen content understanding but also foster critical thinking, digital literacy, and ethical awareness in evolving digital landscapes.

As a second-grade teacher, the author wove collaborative digital storytelling into many subjects and units, including English Language Arts projects exploring the lives of well-known authors. Each student was responsible for researching and drafting a script overviewing a segment of the featured author's life, with the opportunity to illustrate their part of the script. These illustrations were digitized and uploaded into a video creation tool, where each student narrated their respective segment. The final product, which included text, narration, images, and music, showcased a genuine collaborative learning experience that the students and their teacher repeatedly enjoyed watching. This memorable assignment enabled them to produce a collaborative artifact that left a lasting impression on students, the teacher, and even audiences beyond the walls of the classroom.

At the author's university, she oversees the Bachelor of Science and Master of Science programs in Learning, Technology, and Design, designing courses that emphasize authentic, real-world assessment. These programs aim to prepare future instructional designers and educational leaders with the expertise and abilities necessary for transformative leadership in today's evolving academic and professional environments. Instead of textbooks, students access all required materials, including articles, websites, and videos, through the program's learning management system. This ensures that resources remain consistently updated and relevant throughout their studies.

The Learning, Technology, and Design courses exclude quizzes and tests; instead, they emphasize genuine learning experiences connected to students' current or future professions. In every course, learners produce artifacts that address defined learning outcomes. This approach enables students to appreciate the journey of creating completed projects that can be easily and immediately utilized in their workplaces.

For instance, in the "Current Topics in Learning with Technology" course, students engage with adaptive technologies by creating video tutorials. These tutorials highlight the features and applications of an adaptive learning tool suitable for their professional settings. After sharing their videos in a discussion board forum, students watch and give feedback on their peers' tutorials. This collaborative effort helps them compile a valuable collection of original video content. Furthermore, they experience reciprocal learning by sharing innovative applications of adaptive technologies. Through their comments and questions posted to the discussion board, students actively reflect on their insights and learning processes.

The programs' courses equip current and aspiring instructional designers across diverse settings with knowledge and skills they can apply to their immediate or future careers and personal pursuits. Every course is deliberately designed to incorporate real-world learning opportunities that equip students for purposeful careers in schools, businesses, nonprofit sectors, and government entities. Assessments feature a written description along with a video explanation, designed to help students understand the reasoning behind each assignment. Sample artifacts of learning created by past students motivate current students to start with clear objectives, fostering purposefulness and excellence as they work toward their goals.

Student evaluations indicate that learners truly value the chance to participate in applicable, creative learning experiences:

- "I definitely was worried about this class at first because I'm not great with technology, but [our professor] simplified each assignment and made it so easy to excel in the course! I also like how this course is project-based. I tend to forget information quickly after taking a test, so I love that this course allowed me to explore information in a way that allowed me to be creative, thus making me retain more..."
- "I enjoyed your class! I was able to take my teaching experience (finishing my 5th year in education) and apply it to my assignments.... Thank you for a great class!"
- "Not only did she give us the tools and resources we needed, but she delivers the course content in a way that helps us apply it in the real world!! AMAZING!!"
- "Dr. Alaniz is definitely a 'breath of fresh air' for those of us who are not that savvy with technology. She has made it so that we are able to learn new, fun, creative things to make our teaching in whatever field we are in a more gratifying and fulfilling profession that not only benefits us in this ever-changing digital world but also benefits our students and those that we instruct!"
- "I learned a lot that could be applied to my work, and I felt that every assignment was relevant to the course's objectives."

- "I enjoyed this course, especially because it was mostly learner-centered and practical. It aligned well with my career aspirations and allowed me to reflect on my coaching style and apply what I've learned into my work."
- "Thank you for thoroughly explaining the purpose of the course. I have learned quite a bit."
- "Don't change anything. Everything was perfect! This course is very informative and useful in real-world applications. Your approach to facilitating the course should be the model or standard for all educators."
- "I would not change anything about this course. This is one of the most organized and engaging courses I have taken. I take pride in my schoolwork, and this allowed me to have physical proof of my hard work that I can use in the future."
- "She truly cares about the success of her students and makes sure that students always understand how each assignment can be beneficial to them in the future. There is never an assignment/project assigned without purpose. Dr. Alaniz assigns challenging assignments while providing all the information and resources needed to complete them and does everything in her power to set each student up for success."
- "This course was wonderful… I found the coursework both engaging and challenging, and I especially enjoyed that the materials created within this course could be used within my own teaching career. It never felt like completing work for the sake of completing work…"
- "I enjoyed that this class had direct application within our work or teaching environment. I was able to use what I created in this class directly within my own teaching and reflect on it in practice, which I really enjoyed…"
- "I felt that I learned many valuable skills and produced artifacts that I was proud to include in my digital portfolio. I always appreciate the ways in which [our professor] always makes her assignments directly applicable to the work we all do outside of the course…"
- "Thank you for another great course! I was so grateful to learn about and practice collegial coaching and appreciate that we all had the freedom to implement these experiences in a way that worked best for each person's situation…"

As explained by Wang (2017),

> *When teachers are motivated to teach, and students are motivated to learn, the classroom becomes a very pleasant environment. Students are subsequently more able to enjoy the learning process and become more engaged in the classroom. This creates a very positive learning environment where knowledge construction is enthusiastically facilitated by the teacher and joyfully engaged in by students. (p. 4)*

As education advances further into the age of artificial intelligence, its most profound purpose remains unchanged: to ignite curiosity, cultivate purpose, and elevate the human spirit, reminding each learner that while technology may enhance learning, it is their humanity that gives it meaning.

Essential Ideas to Remember

Today's educators must embrace authentic learning to ensure students remain engaged and genuinely involved in their educational journeys. Authentic learning connects classroom tasks to real-world scenarios, encouraging students to take on roles and solve problems that mirror their future careers. This approach, which integrates collaboration, self-assessment, and reflection, allows students to produce meaningful work, fostering excitement and a sense of purpose. Integrating digital tools, including AI, supports personalized learning by adapting to individual needs, thereby allowing teachers to devote more time to mentoring and building relationships with their students. As a result, students feel more supported, confident, and motivated to pursue learning beyond their academic journeys.

Authentic learning not only enhances students' engagement but also revitalizes the teaching process, offering educators the satisfaction of seeing their students grow creatively. By moving away from traditional assessments like tests and quizzes, educators can cultivate an environment where students explore their interests and develop skills applicable to their future endeavors. This approach fosters joy in learning, making the classroom a dynamic space where both educators and students are motivated to create and innovate.

Through real-world assignments like digital storytelling, students develop a sense of accomplishment and connection to their learning, while educators experience the fulfillment of facilitating these transformative experiences.

What greater gift could an educator, or their students, hope to achieve? By embracing authentic learning, educators hold the power to profoundly impact their classroom learning environments—and, even more significantly, to transform students' lives for years to come.

References

Amoush, S.A. and A. Farhat (2023, December 13). "The Power of Authentic Assessment in the Age of AI." *Faculty Focus*. Available online: https://www.facultyfocus.com/articles/educational-assessment/the-power-of-authentic-assessment-in-the-age-of-ai/.

Gravett, K., C.A. Taylor, and N. Fairchild (2024). "Pedagogies of Mattering: Re-conceptualising Relational Pedagogies in Higher Education." *Teaching in Higher Education*, 29(2): 388–403.

Moquin, S. (2024, November 26). "Ethical Considerations for AI Use in Education." *Enrollify*. Available online: https://www.enrollify.org/blog/ethical-considerations-for-ai-use-in-education.

Timperley, C. and K. Schick (2025). "Assessment as Pedagogy: Inviting Authenticity Through Relationality, Vulnerability, and Wonder." *Teaching in Higher Education*, 30(3): 592–607.

Wang, C.K.J. (2017). "The Joy of Learning: What Is It and How to Achieve It." *Exchange*, 1: 7–11.

About the Author

Katie Alaniz, EdD, serves as Associate Dean for the College of Education and Behavioral Sciences Online and Director of the Center for Learning Innovations and Teaching Excellence (C-LITE) at Houston Christian University, where she also teaches undergraduate and graduate education courses. As a teacher and digital learning specialist for over two decades in both public and private schools, Dr. Alaniz guides educators as they meaningfully integrate digital tools and resources within their classrooms. She has authored or co-authored a number of books, including *Naturalizing Digital Immigrants: The Power of Collegial Coaching for Technology Integration*; *Digital Media in Today's Classroom: The Potential for Meaningful Teaching, Learning, and Assessment*; *Collegial Coaching: Mentoring for Knowledge and Skills That Transfer to Real-World Applications*; *The Maximizer Mindset: Work Less, Achieve More, Spread Joy*; *Authentic Assessment in Action: An Everyday Guide for Bringing Learning to Life through Meaningful Assessment*; and *A Learning Community Built on Strengths: Inspiring Educators to Positively Impact Student Lives*. Additionally, she has published academic articles on a range of topics, presented at a variety of educational conferences in the United States and abroad, and delivered a TEDx Talk. Her primary research interests include authentic assessment, digital learning, artificial intelligence in education, collegial coaching, and teacher education. Dr. Alaniz and her husband, Steven, reside in Seabrook, Texas.

www.ingramcontent.com/pod-product-compliance
Ingram Content Group UK Ltd.
Pitfield, Milton Keynes, MK11 3LW, UK
UKHW020648110926
475431UK00001B/51

9 781475 875027